T0208312

A Life God
REWARDS

❧ BIBLE STUDY ❧

LEADER'S EDITION

BRUCE WILKINSON

WITH DAVID KOPP

Multnomah Books

A LIFE GOD REWARDS BIBLE STUDY LEADER'S EDITION
published by Multnomah Books

© 2002 by Exponential, Inc.
International Standard Book Number 9781590528266

Cover image by Koechel Peterson & Associates

Scripture is from *The Holy Bible,* New King James Version.
Copyright © 1982 by Thomas Nelson, Inc. Used by permission.

Other Scripture quotations:
The Holy Bible, New International Version (NIV)
© 1973, 1984 by International Bible Society,
used by permission of Zondervan Publishing House

Published in the United States by WaterBrook Multnomah, an imprint of the Crown
Publishing Group, a division of Random House Inc., New York.

MULTNOMAH and its mountain colophon are registered trademarks of Random House Inc.

For information:
MULTNOMAH BOOKS
12265 ORACLE BOULEVARD, SUITE 200
COLORADO SPRINGS, CO 80921

146651086

DEAR BIBLE STUDY LEADER,

Welcome to an awesome and important task—helping men and women in our generation see the connection between what they're doing today for God and how He will reward them in eternity. By accepting this challenge, you're taking a stand with followers of Jesus through the ages who have carefully listened to what He said about eternity. How much impact your work as a study leader will have in eternity will never be known...until the day we are home with Him. And then it will be plain for all to see!

May you sense God's pleasure and favor in your life as you faithfully serve Him with your class. Solomon wrote that God put eternity in the hearts of every person (Ecclesiastes 3:11). Undoubtedly, one of the things Jesus did best was to help people who were caught up in their ordinary lives "see through to eternity." May you be blessed by His presence and power as you strive to help others make the same life-changing breakthrough.

SEEING THROUGH TO ETERNITY

I wrote *A Life God Rewards* because I became convinced that what Jesus said about the importance of our work for Him—and what He would do in eternity in response—was being almost completely overlooked in our time. The book is based primarily on Jesus' own words—what He said about good works, what God expects from His servants, the promise of eternal reward, the judgment of believers, and our life in heaven. The teachings of Paul and other apostles on the same subjects add important insight and detail.

If you haven't read *A Life God Rewards,* I urge you to do so before you begin the study. Like *The Prayer of Jabez* and *Secrets of the Vine,* it's a book you can read and enjoy in one evening. For a much deeper treatment, you can study with me in the eight-part video series (www.globalvisionresources.com).

You're going to find an eager audience in your students! Everyone wonders about life after death. Everyone instinctively knows that what we do with our life matters, and that it will matter forever. And everyone, even those who are jaded about church or religion, wants to hear what Jesus had to say about it. You are in for a real treat.

This may be especially true if you're a first-time or inexperienced group leader. In some ways, you have the *most* to look forward to! God used Paul to change the Roman world, yet remember what he wrote: "My speech and my preaching were not with persuasive words of human wisdom, but in demonstration of the Spirit and of power, that your faith should not be in the wisdom of men but in the power of God" (1 Corinthians 2:4–5).

Whether you are a first-timer or a veteran, you bring the same essential gifts to class:

♦ the truth of God's Word;

♦ a desire to serve God and help others;

♦ a complete dependence on God to do His work.

As you ask God to use these gifts each week, you'll hear inspiring stories from your students about what they're learning. You'll see God at work changing lives. And you will change too.

ESTABLISHING COMMON GROUND

To get your class on the same page, I strongly recommend that you lead the class in making three commitments:

1. Everyone agrees to read *A Life God Rewards* or listen to the audio book at least once.

2. Everyone commits to spending one to two hours the week before class working through the week's material. Each week is divided into seven study segments to facilitate daily use.

3. Everyone commits to ask God to change their lives according to the truth. After all, this isn't a study *about* eternal reward; it's an invitation to let what Jesus said change you personally.

Another excellent way to enhance your study is to use the thirty-one-day *A Life God Rewards Devotional* and the accompanying *Journal*. These learning tools will take you to a deeper level of understanding eternal rewards. Consider initiating a plan for the whole class to follow the devotional/journal as parallel projects during your four weeks of study.

For other related helps, see Recommended Resources in the general introduction and on page one of each week's study.

STRUCTURE OF EACH SESSION

Each week, the study leads the class through a dynamic, life-changing process:

1. What do you really believe? (personal inventory).

2. Bible study on the main idea for the week (over four weeks you'll explore eternity, reward in heaven, judgment of the believer, and stewarding your life for God).

3. Case studies of key Bible characters that demonstrate the lesson.

4. Practical applications of the theme.

5. Confronting the major hindrances that are preventing life change.

6. Changing your beliefs to conform with the truth.

7. In light of eternity, making a new commitment to serve God each day.

HOW TO TEACH WELL

Pray for your time together each day of the preceding week. Pray for each member of your group by name:

♦ for supernatural blessings from the Holy Spirit.
♦ for spiritual insight into eternal truths.
♦ for personal breakthroughs where they are needed most.
♦ for protection from disunity, quarreling, ill will, and pride.

Prepare thoroughly for each session. Ask God to first change you with the truth. Your confidence will increase directly in proportion to your level of familiarity with the material. Consider asking two friends to track with you through the study; then meet by phone or in person a day or so before your class to talk through any reactions or sticking points. Use a New King James Version Bible if available (not required). Keep a topical concordance or Bible handbook nearby. Take a minute to review the seven distinctives of this study, outlined in the general introduction.

Guide your class time with a firm but sensitive hand. *Remember, there is more material than you will need to or can cover in one week;* your first opportunity is to guide your class through the study in the way that works best for everyone. You are not the answer person; you are the facilitator and encourager. Keep the discussion on topic and as close to your intended schedule as possible. Don't hesitate to redirect the conversation away from dominating persons and pointless arguments. Everyone doesn't have to agree.

The following icons highlight good starting points for lively discussions and will help you know how to order your class time for best results:

 indicates a key verse, definition, or explanation. Use this as a review tool and to make sure that you don't miss the main point.

 *indicates optional material for further study. Use this icon to help you decide what materials you can leave for later. If you have limited time, it's better to do key parts well than to try to rush through all of it.*

 *indicates a group process question that focuses on life experience rather than on the Bible text being addressed.*

Share honestly from your own life, and invite others to do so as well. Talk about what you're learning, or still trying to learn, about the lesson. Keep the discussion focused on personal application, not abstractions.

Expect to see God at work—before, during, and after class—in the lives of your students. God has an important, eternal purpose for each participant.

$$Week\ One$$

THE TRUTH ABOUT
YOUR ETERNITY

Welcome. Welcome your class to a study about how to get the most out of life for today and for eternity.

Ask who has read the book *A Life God Rewards* and what they thought about it. Invite people to share any personal learning goals for today's session. These might be stated as doubts or questions they want answered. Talk about the three class commitments described on page 2.

Getting Started. This is a Bible study that begins at a most important moment in everyone's future. Jesus describes the moment in Matthew 16:27—"For the Son of Man will come in the glory of His Father with His angels, and then He will reward each according to his works."

The most important goal for this week is to help each student reevaluate his life from the perspective of that moment: when Jesus will reward each of us according to what we did for Him.

You might want to read the "Getting Started" paragraphs aloud. Review the week's objectives listed in the "This Week You'll Discover…" box. Then open with prayer.

1. WHAT DO I REALLY BELIEVE ABOUT ETERNITY?

Question 2. You'll find an inventory in the first section of each week of the Bible study. The inventories are intended to help provoke fresh thinking, not to define the problem or be doctrinally comprehensive. Keep this time fun. Ask your class to hold off on in-depth discussions at this point (a lot of questions will be answered as we go along). Invite your group to share inventory results. Ask, *Was anyone surprised?*

2. WHAT WILL HAPPEN IN ETERNITY?

The Timeline of Your Eternity. Students who are familiar with what the Bible says about future events may notice that some were not included, such as the Rapture, the Second Coming, the Tribulation, and the kingdom. That's because this study focuses on a broad view of the events *everyone* will personally experience.

Event #1: Life. [a.] created in the image of God to take care of "every living thing." [b.] spirit, soul, and body.

    Event #2: Death. die; once.

    Event #3: Destination. believes; believe; believed.

    Event #4: Resurrection. body; body or likeness.

    Event # 5: Repayment. appear; receive; good; bad. This event, which is the focus of this study, may come as a surprise to some in the group. Assure those who have questions that we'll be studying this event a great deal in the weeks to come. At this point, students may ask about the great white throne judgment mentioned in Revelation 20:11–13. Opinions in the church vary on this point. Many Christians believe that only Christians will stand before the bema of Jesus, and that the Revelation passage refers to a separate judgment for nonbelievers. Others believe that the Scriptures indicate one judgment for everyone. Encourage students to focus on the clear biblical truth that every person—including every Christian—will stand before Jesus to give an account of His life.

Event #6: Eternity. *[a.]* punishment; life, *[b.]* mansions, He will prepare a place, He will come again, His followers will be with Him.

3. WHAT WILL MATTER IN ETERNITY?

Question 1. *[a.]* belief, *[b.]* The First Key: My belief/faith determines my eternal destination. **Note:** This might be a good time to make sure all your students understand the message of salvation and feel confident about their eternal destination. If some don't, offer to meet with them privately; suggest they read (or reread) chapter 7 of *A Life God Rewards* in preparation.

Question 2. *[a.]* works, *[b.]* The Second Key: My behavior/works determine my eternal compensation (or reward).

Question 4. workmanship; good works.

"Comparing the Two Keys to My Eternity" Chart. Great confusion exists around the world and in the church when it comes to the roles of works and faith. I see two common errors:

1. The error of Christians is to say, "Works don't matter; only what you believe matters." This error is based on a misapplication of a wonderful truth: that Jesus did the work of salvation for us by paying the penalty for our sin on Calvary. But Jesus' work of salvation for us does not mean that our work for Him has no significance.

2. The error of many other religions around the world is to teach, "Enough good works will gain you entrance into heaven."

The truth is that while no amount of works can achieve our salvation, works do matter greatly to God and will determine much about how we spend our eternity.

4. WHAT IS THE SURPRISING TRUTH ABOUT HEAVEN?

Questions 1–2. "according to."

Question 3. Greater service to God on earth will be rewarded by more reward—in this case, greater opportunity to serve and have authority—in heaven. It follows, then, that our experience in heaven will vary, depending upon how we have served God on earth.

Question 4. Faithfulness over a few things on earth will be rewarded with rule "over many things" in heaven.

Talk Point and "Wonderful for All" Box. The truth that heaven won't be experienced in the same way by every child of God may raise objections among your students. Because we live in a fallen, sinful world, it's hard for us to envision authority administered without abuse, or how varying rewards could not provoke envy or resentment. Reassure your students with these key truths:

♦ Heaven will be equally home for all God's children (John 14:2–3).
♦ We will be with Jesus and be resurrected in His likeness (1 John 3:2).
♦ We will all see God's greatness, justice, and goodness, and we will all joyfully worship Him (Revelation 15:3–4).
♦ In heaven, no one will experience want, suffering, envy or striving or sin of any kind because the curse of sin will be removed (Revelation 21:2–5).

5. WHAT IS THE SURPRISING TRUTH ABOUT HELL?

Question 1. Qualifiers like "more tolerable" and "greater" indicate that there will be different levels of retribution or punishment in hell for differing degrees of wickedness on earth.

Question 2. "Treasuring up for yourself wrath" shows that, in the same way that good works for God store up reward in heaven for the believer, evil deeds store up punishment in hell for the unbeliever. When we see inequity and injustice all around us every day, it is comforting to know that one day Jesus *will* make everything just and right. In fact, the idea that a mass murderer will receive greater punishment than my well-intentioned neighbor who doesn't believe in Jesus seems fair—and even reassuring—to most people.

Talk Point. None of us wants to pass judgment on who will or will not receive reward or punishment. Besides being keenly aware of our own failings, we don't want to appear sanctimonious or judgmental. Hell—the overwhelming torment, finality, and eternity of it—is extremely sobering.

Extra: "The Beggar and the Rich Man." Neither Lazarus nor the rich man questioned God's judgment. Verse 25 shows justice in eternity. Also, Abraham reminds the rich man that God has already sent the law and the prophets to testify of the truth. Paul wrote, "Since the creation of the world His invisible attributes are clearly seen, being understood by the things that are made…so that they are without excuse" (Romans 1:20).

6. HOW SHOULD I THINK ABOUT ETERNITY TODAY?

Question 1. [a.] Dr. Earl Radmacher, president emeritus of Western Seminary, uses this saying in his teaching on eternal reward: "Now is a day of change; then is a day of no change. Now is a day of becoming; then is a day of being what I have become for all eternity." *[b.]* What I believe and what I do.

Question 2. Consequence—or the laws of cause and effect—are not only a universal reality, they are a requirement for positive achievement in many arenas. Positive consequences of eternal reward include: *1.)* showing us the importance of our good works to God; *2.)* demonstrating His generosity and justice; *3.)* reinforcing the significance of our brief time on earth; *4.)* motivating us to live our lives more completely and to serve God more fully.

7. WHAT COULD KEEP ME FROM LIVING WITH ETERNITY IN MIND?

Allow your class time to process their responses privately. Ask them to choose one or two of the reasons that seem to be their greatest obstacles. They can then look up the corresponding references and write out a new breakthrough belief. Afterward, invite them to share comments or personal insights. This discussion can lead naturally into a time of prayer and commitment.

1. The "Big Blur" Belief. See answer for Event #6, *[b.],* page 11.
2. The "New to Me" Resistance. The Bereans searched the Bible to find the truth or error of new teachings; then they changed their beliefs; then they acted.
3. The "Socialism" Stalemate. God is eternal; God is in control; God will judge with justice; God is good.
4. The "Love Is All You Need" Defense. Jesus linked genuine love and service with meaningful good works. If we say we love Him, but don't do what He asks, our words are empty.

IN CLOSING...

Ask your group how they're feeling about the material and the pacing of the class. How could the learning experience be improved for next week? As a send-off, ask your students to draw the illustration of the dot and the line and post it where they can see it every day in the coming week. Encourage them to spend time on next week's lesson.

Week Two

THE GOOD NEWS ABOUT REWARDS

Welcome. Report on the week: "How much time did you spend thinking about eternity last week? How did the illustration of the dot and the line impact your thinking? Has last week's lesson changed your choices or attitudes?"
Getting Started. Read the introductory text aloud and review the week's objectives listed in the "This Week You'll Discover..." box. Then open with prayer.

1. WHAT DO I BELIEVE ABOUT ETERNAL REWARDS?

Question 2. Inventory. Invite your group to share results. Does anyone find it difficult to believe that all these statements are false? If any of the statements ring true to students, discuss how they arrived at this belief.

2. WHAT DID JESUS REVEAL ABOUT ETERNAL REWARDS?

Question 1. [a.] heaven, [b.] rejoice, glad; rejoice, joy.
Question 2. [a.] repaid (or repay), [b.] resurrection.
Question 3. [a.] Notice Jesus didn't scold Peter for his self-concern. Obviously, Jesus thought this was a legitimate and appropriate question. There's more discussion about the topic of motivation in "The 'Motivation Situation' Mix-Up" on page 33 of this week. [b.] A "hundredfold" is equal to a 10,000-percent return! The potential rewards of heaven are obviously great in value. And since they will last for all eternity, we can hardly compare them to the kind of fleeting temporal rewards we might receive on earth. [c.] When we consider how generously God plans to reward us, suddenly we begin to view our work for God not as a great sacrifice on our part— but as an amazing opportunity to work for a faithful and generous Lord.
Question 5. [a.] heaven, [b.] works, [c.] great; hundred, [d.] joy.
Talk Point. Jesus spoke most often about the rewards that will come to us in heaven. However, godly living can also bring enormous temporal benefit in our lives on earth (this is the emphasis of the whole book of Proverbs). And God rewards us both "in this time" and "in the age to come" (Mark 10:30). Encourage your class to list some of the blessings or rewards that come to us now as a result of obedience. Then discuss what might happen if a person expected all or even most of his reward for good works to come in the here and now. (We might begin to doubt God's faithfulness and lose heart when we don't see immediate benefits from our efforts.)

3. WHAT DOES "REWARD" MEAN IN THE BIBLE?

Question 1. [a.] wages, [b.] wages, [c.] wages, [d.] reward, [e.] reward, [f.] reward.
Question 2. A token of appreciation is usually less than what the work was worth— and is meant as a thank-you. A tip is usually given over and above the payment for a work—as a bonus or gesture of gratitude for a job well done. But both the tip and token are optional on the part of the giver, not guaranteed or promised.
Talk Point. [1.] Assure your class that accepting what Jesus said about His reward doesn't mean that they must always think of, or relate to, God as "boss." He is also Creator, Provider, Friend, and Redeemer, for example. [2.] Some students might welcome the idea of being paid "wages"—especially if they are actively serving God and have often wondered why God doesn't bless them more for their work now.

Question 3. *[a.]* repay, *[b.]* render, *[c.]* repaid, *[d.]* reward, *[e.]* reward.

Box: Do You Have to Believe in Reward? In the Hebrews 11:6 reference, don't let your class be thrown off by the clause that ends the verse—"that He is a rewarder of *those who diligently seek Him.*" This phrase is commonly assumed to refer to any sort of general spiritual interest or feeling. Yet the powerful testimony of the rest of Hebrews 11 shows us that the belief of these seekers compelled them both to *know* the will of God and to *do* it, against great odds. God rewards our actions (which are the genuine proof of our faith), not our feelings.

4. WHAT ARE "GOOD WORKS"?

Question 1. *[a.]* fruit; fruit *[b.]* much.
Question 2. good works; unfruitful.
Question 3. good works.
Talk Point. Often we mistake attending a social occasion, doing charity work for personal benefit, or having a nice feeling during worship for "good works." We define good works in terms of eternal reward more completely on the next page, and in next week (in day 5, "What will endure the fire at the bema?").

5. WHAT SPECIFIC WORKS WILL GOD REWARD?

Question 1. If time is short, you might assign each question to a different student and then fill in the blanks together.

SCRIPTURES	What Present Behavior IS COMMANDED?	What Future Result IS PROMISED?
I TIMOTHY 6:18–19	Do good works, be ready to give, willing to share	"storing up for themselves a good foundation"
COLOSSIANS 3:23–24	Serve your master "as to the Lord"	The reward of the inheritance
LUKE 6:35	Love your enemies, do good, lend freely	Reward will be great
MATTHEW 6:3–4	Charitable deeds	Reward openly
MATTHEW 6:6	Pray in secret	Reward openly
MATTHEW 6:17–18	Fast in private	Reward openly

Question 2. *[a.]* hungry; fed *[b.]* thirsty; gave drink *[c.]* stranger; took in *[d.]* naked; clothed *[e.]* sick; visited *[f.]* in prison; came.

6. WHO ARE SOME BIBLE PEOPLE THAT LIVED FOR REWARD?

Moses, Prince of Egypt. Question 1. looked to the reward.
Question 2. Obviously, Moses would not make the sacrifices he did unless he thought the reward would be real, guaranteed, and highly desirable.
Paul, Witness to Kings. Question 1. *[a.]* in such a way that you may obtain it, *[b.]* an imperishable crown.

Question 2. *[a.]* uncertainty, *[b.]* discipline.
Question 3. Becoming disqualified for his reward or crown.
Talk Point. Paul ran for the prize (Philippians 3:12–15).

7. WHAT IS KEEPING ME FROM WANTING ETERNAL REWARD?

Read the opening text aloud, then encourage the class to take a few minutes to process the page privately. Ask them to choose one or two of the attitudes or beliefs that are their greatest obstacles, respond to the teaching, and write out their new belief. Afterward, invite them to share comments or personal insights.

When the class seems ready, suggest that the group pray the prayer of commitment on the last page together.

Week Three

THE GOOD NEWS OF THE BEMA

Welcome. Your class has reached the halfway point in this important study. This is a good time to visually look at the four parts of the study: eternity, rewards, the bema, and living for eternity. Then ask some review questions about last week's study.

The most important goal for today's lesson is that your class comes to grips with two huge truths: *1)* Every believer will stand before the judgment seat of Christ, and *2)* that day is meant to be the best day of a Christian's life!

1. WHAT DO I BELIEVE ABOUT GOD'S JUDGMENT?

Question 1. The idea is to begin to think about what it means to stand before a judge—and how your future at that moment depends both on your past actions and on the character and understanding of the judge.
Question 2. Inventory. All of the statements on the inventory are false. If students are tempted to argue with results, agree to revisit the inventory after the class has completed the week's lessons. But if most of your class scored high on the inventory, ask if there are some statements they might have believed were true a month ago. How and why has their thinking changed?
Talk Point. An awareness that we will be accountable changes how we think and what we do. Would students' lives change a little, or dramatically? How do most of us cope with knowing that God sees and knows everything about us?

2. WILL CHRISTIANS BE ACCOUNTABLE IN ETERNITY?

Question 1. *[a.]* Jesus, *[b.]* 100 percent, *[c.]* an account of our lives, *[d.]* Have the class make a list of traits drawn from these passages. Begin with the line, "Jesus is the best Person to evaluate my life because _____."

Question 2. *[a.]* all, *[b.]* Jesus, *[c.]* individuals, *[d.]* alive, *[e.]* not.

Talk Point. The judgment seat of Christ has been an accepted part of church teachings throughout history. Scholars point out, however, that the truths of the bema and rewards tend to have greater meaning to followers of Jesus during times when the church is undergoing persecution. During times of prosperity, the message often falls by the wayside.

3. WHAT WILL HAPPEN AT THE BEMA?

Question 1. *[a.]* clear; declare; revealed by fire, *[b.]* test; work, *[c.]* valuable and enduring, *[d.]* worthless; short-lived, *[e.]* reward.

Question 2. *[a.]* the crown of righteousness, *[b.]* all who love His appearing (look forward to His return).

4. HOW CAN I "SUFFER LOSS" AT THE BEMA?

Question 1. do; works.

Question 2. has everlasting.

Question 3. *[a.]* perfected forever, *[b.]* no more.

LOSS IN HEAVEN

Question 1. Although our sins will not be revisited or punished at the bema, they will still affect the outcome. That is because when we sin, we damage ourselves, others, and ultimately our work for God. Some examples: a church leader who is caught embezzling money; a teenager who witnesses at school but is seen abusing drugs on Friday night; a busy mom who begins to put her friends and social life ahead of her family. None of these will receive the full reward for the good work they were engaged in. A second way we "suffer loss" is by forfeiting potential rewards. When we pursue a sinful activity, we aren't pursuing the kind of good works that will be rewarded. Ask your students to comment on these two ways of "losing" at the bema.

Question 2. Ask for volunteers to share their answer.

Question 3. Refer back to the scenarios described for *Question 1.* As we saw in the book *Secrets of the Vine,* three ways God is at work to increase our fruitfulness for Him are: *a.)* disciplining us for sin; *b.)* pruning our priorities; and *c.)* inviting us to abide more fully in relationship with Him. These three areas suggest many practical steps class members could take to avoid loss at the bema.

5. WHAT WILL ENDURE THE FIRE AT THE BEMA?

Question 1. *[a.]* great, *[b.]* nothing.
Question 2. *[a.]* nothing, *[b.]* the Holy Spirit.
Question 3. *[a.]* none, *[b.]* in secret.
Question 4. *[a.]* will; Father, *[b.]* We look out for our own interests, not God's.
Talk Point. God never intended for us to run around trying to rack up good works at random. When we stay in close relationship with God, the natural result is that we work in His strength and are able to discern His will for us—those specific good works He planned for us and puts in our path.

6. HOW WILL GOD REWARD ME FOR WORKS THAT ENDURE?

Question 1. *[a.]* judging, *[b.]* honor.
Question 2. *[a.]* glory, *[b.]* crown of life, *[c.]* crown of righteousness, *[d.]* crown of rejoicing.
"Will I Give My Crowns Back to Jesus?" Some students may resist giving up what may be a cherished idea that they will give their rewards back to Christ. Try to help them understand by proposing the following hypothetical situation:

Your son has done well in high school and is about to begin his new life at college. You want to reward him for his efforts. You buy him a carload of things you know will benefit him at school—a computer and software to go with it, a hot plate for his room, a beanbag chair, a floor lamp to read by…but instead of appreciating your generosity, he insists that you keep your gifts. He says he is too grateful to accept them and knows he couldn't have gotten where he is without you. How would you feel?

Like any loving parent, God can't wait to reward you! His rewards will be valuable and meant to be enjoyed by you for all eternity. In fact, as we'll see next week, His rewards will make the life He wants to give you in heaven possible.

7. WHAT'S KEEPING ME FROM LIVING FOR THE DAY WHEN I STAND BEFORE JESUS?

Read the opening text aloud, then encourage the class to take a few minutes to process the page privately. Ask them to choose one or two of the attitudes or beliefs that are their greatest obstacles, look up the Scripture, and write out their new belief. Afterward, invite them to share comments or personal "ahas."

Week Four

LIVING FOR GOD'S "WELL DONE!"

<u>Welcome.</u> Report on the week. Invite comments about last week's exploration of the believer's judgment and about preparation for this week's study of how we can live for God's "Well done!" This entire Bible study should radically enlarge your class's understanding of God's extravagant grace—His grace in saving us is unmerited, immeasurable and *amazing!* And His grace in rewarding us for serving Him is unmerited, immeasurable…and *amazing!*

<u>Getting Started.</u> Read the introductory story aloud. Review the week's objectives. Then open with prayer, asking God to show each person present a new way to live every day—the way that will result in "great reward" for all eternity.

1. WHAT DO I THINK MY LIFE IS WORTH?

<u>Question 1.</u> Stewardship isn't a word we use much these days, but it describes a powerful idea that Jesus spoke about often in His parables. We usually associate stewardship with money, but this week we use it in a much larger sense. A steward in the Bible is a special kind of servant—one who is:

♦ entrusted to manage his master's assets
♦ in his master's best interests
♦ while his master is away.

<u>Talk Point.</u> An asset is anything of worth that can be used to create more value. Your assets might include your talents, time, skills, social or economic position, finances, personality strengths, family background, spiritual gifts, etc. Get the class thinking in terms of what God has entrusted them with on earth—anything they could use to help grow His kingdom.

2. WHAT SHOULD I DO WITH MY TIME AND TALENTS?

<u>Portrait of a Steward.</u> <u>Question 1.</u> The steward's opportunity to work for reward is after his master has commissioned him and gone away, and before he returns.

<u>Question 2.</u> If your students are unsure of the answer, ask them to pay special attention to verse 11. The disciples still expected Jesus to set up His kingdom on earth. But Jesus wanted them to know that He would soon be going away—and the business of His kingdom on earth would be delegated to them. They would be commissioned to spend their lives greatly increasing His kingdom. In the future He would return, ask for an accounting, and reward His servants.

Question 3. Identify the great commission, and be sure your students understand that as Christians today we are in the same circumstances as the disciples were about to find themselves in—our Master is away, and we have been commissioned to "do business" with what He has given us until He returns.

Talk Point. Many of us take *better* care of something if it belongs to another, especially if that person is extremely important to us. And we keep in mind an important fact— the owner *will* return and *will* expect a good report.

THREE SERVANTS, THREE STORIES

Question 1. [a.] 1; 10, [b.] good servant, [c.] little; 10.
Question 2. [a.] 1; 5, [b.] 5, [c.] Well done, good servant.
Question 3. [a.] 1; 1, [b.] wicked, [c.] Take. **Note:** Point out that because he wasn't praised in the same way as the first servant, the master must have known that the second servant could have done more than he did. Postpone any discussion on the third servant until the next page.
Question 4. [a.] God, [b.] multiply, [c.] reward, [d.] loss.

3. HOW MUCH DOES GOD EXPECT FROM MY LIFE?

Question 1. huge returns; little or no return.
Question 2. Give your students a couple of minutes to think about and answer this question. It's a fun way to imagine how we reinterpret what God asks of us in order to "downsize" His assignment to our level of willingness to work.

Talk Point. [1.] Some other ways to ponder this question: "Do you think most Christians see nothing really wrong with hiding or merely 'sitting on' their talents and gifts?" "What common rationalizations do you hear or have you given?" [2.] Some students may object to the idea that God cares about results. Assure them that this doesn't mean He doesn't care about effort. The two together—effort and a commitment to getting results—describe faithful stewardship. Yet what will be measured at the bema is *what we did,* not what we wanted or intended to do. Paul said, "Moreover it is required in stewards that one be found faithful" (1 Corinthians 4:2).

DIFFERENT ABILITY, EQUAL OPPORTUNITY

Question 3. [a.] same; same, [b.] he loses it.
Question 4. reward; potential.
Question 5. Because God's requirements of us take into account what we have been given to work with, we can make three key statements:
- We are all equally commissioned.
- We are each differently gifted.
- We all have an equal opportunity to receive God's commendation and reward.

Extra: The First Church. These believers depended on the power of the Holy Spirit; they understood that they were commissioned to reach the whole world; they witnessed with passion; they practiced unity, fellowship, and sharing of possessions; they took care of each other's needs; they praised often; they cultivated favor in the community; they delegated responsibilities according to giftedness and opportunity.

4. WHAT SHOULD I DO WITH MY TREASURE?

Question 1. *[a.]* moth; rust; thieves, *[c.]* not; treasures; earth.

Question 2. *[a.]* lay up, *[b.]* yourselves, *[c.]* heaven.

Question 3. Some of us feel a flicker of resentment every time an offering plate or appeal for money comes our way. But Jesus revealed that giving is the only method of long-term "keeping." Paul spoke about this principle to the Philippians: "Now you Philippians know also that in the beginning of the gospel, when I departed from Macedonia, no church shared with me concerning giving and receiving but you only. For even in Thessalonica you sent aid once and again for my necessities. *Not that I seek the gift, but I seek the fruit that abounds to your account*" (Philippians 4:15–17, emphasis added).

Talk Point. When Jesus speaks of treasure in heaven, many believers are tempted to conclude that Jesus wasn't talking about literal treasure. They assume He was referring to some kind of vague, undefinable spiritual benefit. But significantly, Jesus used exactly the same word *(thesauros)* to describe treasure in heaven as treasure on earth.

5. HOW DO I MOVE MY TREASURE FROM EARTH TO HEAVEN?

Question 1. Sell all you have and give to the poor.

Question 2. sell; give; treasure; fail.

Question 3. The words *foundation for the time to come* indicate that treasure in heaven will be important—something we will build on.

Question 5. Scripture teaches that we should tithe first of all to our church. Giving above and beyond that, students would be wise to consider what kind of return for God's kingdom their "investment" will produce.

6. HOW IS FAITHFUL STEWARDSHIP REWARDED IN ETERNITY?

Question 1. To be found faithful.

Question 2. unrighteous mammon; true. **Note:** *Mammon* is another word for money. Unlike earthly money, treasure in heaven will not be subject to corruption, greed, or misuse. It will be used for noble purposes and will bring only good.

Question 3. faithful; given.

Question 4. All our money and possessions are on loan from God.

Question 5. Positions of authority or responsibility—in other words, more opportunities to serve God. The degree to which we serve God well on earth is the degree to which we will be privileged to serve Him in heaven. And serving Him as meaningfully as possible is what we will most desire to do. This is why the disciples were anxious to earn positions to His left or right in heaven (Matthew 20:21–23).

Question 6. Willingness to serve.

Talk Point. To begin your discussion, you might want to share this quote from David Lloyd George, a British prime minister from the early twentieth century:

> *When I was a boy, the thought of heaven used to frighten me more than the thought of hell. I pictured heaven as a place where time would be perpetual Sundays, with perpetual services from which there would be no escape. It was a horrible nightmare...and made me an atheist for ten years.*

Ask for reaction to this quote. Now is a good time to remind your group that how we think about heaven is reflected in how we live out our lives on earth. That's because our whole life on earth can be seen as a preparation for a life, not just an existence, in heaven.

Biblical descriptions of heaven are full of concrete images—cities, trees, houses, animals, and people. In addition to worship, the Bible points to many other activities in heaven—people there enjoy, eat, and rest. They have possessions. They have relationships with recognizable people. They feel joy and pleasure. They are in every way deeply involved with their surroundings. And those surroundings are supremely beautiful—walls of precious stones, gates of pearl, pavement of gold.

God wanted us to know that heaven is a real place that is so wonderful it will make our lives on earth pale in comparison.

Passages for further study: Luke 22:29–30; John 14:2–4; Hebrews 12:22–24; Revelation 14:12–13; 19:8–9; 21:21; and 22:2–4.

7. WHAT'S KEEPING ME FROM A LIFE GOD REWARDS?

LIVING FOR WHAT LASTS

This is an important time of review, reevaluation, and commitment. Be sure to leave time for students to process. Don't be afraid of silence. When the time is right, help your group share any personal reflections or commitments. Then proceed to closing.

IN CLOSING...

When your class is ready, have them sign the pledge and close the class in prayer. You may choose to read the closing prayer together.

Thank your class for the time and effort they've invested in this important study. You may want to suggest follow-up options for individuals or groups:

♦ Find an accountability partner who will help you continue to process Jesus' teaching on eternal reward and integrate it into your life.

♦ Form a "ten-mina group" of members who want to look for ways to greatly increase the results of their lives for God.

Introduction

THE AMAZING LINK

What if I told you that your actions today could actually change what you experience after you die...and keep on changing it forever? Would that possibility surprise you?

The truth is, Jesus revealed a direct and powerful link between what we do for God today and how He will reward us in heaven. The Bible study you're holding—based on the book *A Life God Rewards*—could be the most life-transforming study you've ever undertaken, because it carefully explores what God said on this vital subject. I promise that once you understand how much your life is supposed to add up for God's glory and your eternal reward, you'll never look at any day as ordinary again.

Unfortunately, among followers of Jesus today there is widespread confusion about the importance of our work for God. Many think that their *belief* is all that matters, and that once they've received the gift of eternal life, any *works* for God are not very important. Many Christians believe, in fact, that what they do on earth has no effect on their eternity.

Could you be one?

Jesus came to show us something else entirely. Jesus revealed that you and I have been more than saved *from* something; we have been saved *to* something—an amazing destiny of serving Him and enjoying His favor.

And it is supposed to start right now.

YOUR GOD IS A REWARDER

Jesus spread the news of reward in heaven in His first major teaching, the Sermon on the Mount. He talked about its certainty with His disciples in private. And He shocked the religious experts of His day with its promise.

As you'll discover in this study, Jesus urgently wanted His followers to know that whatever good works they did for God would reap a tangible and significant reward from Him in eternity…and that they had been created and called to do *a lot of good works* for Him!

Jesus was both direct and specific in what He revealed. For example:

A DIFFERENT KIND OF BIBLE STUDY

The four-week Bible study you're holding invites you to go deeply into God's Word to see what Jesus and the apostles taught about eternal rewards. We adhere to the key doctrines and beliefs that followers of Christ have historically affirmed. Besides being biblically based and felt-needs oriented, the study has several key distinctives:

It's topical. We focus on the biblical support in key areas—our life in eternity, the rewards Jesus promised, the believer's judgment at the bema, and defining a productive life of service God can reward.

It's conversation friendly. Some questions are information based. Some are intended simply to provoke a helpful discussion.

It's designed for individual or group use. Each week is broken down into seven major segments (see the numbered questions at the top of the page). Students can use these for a daily study plan, if they wish.

It's question driven. Sometimes called the Socratic method, this teaching method pulls you from topic to topic through a sequence of key questions.

It incorporates several learning approaches. You'll find inductive studies, fill-in-the-blanks, personal inventories, character profiles, Bible exposition, and inspiring quotes.

It offers plenty of options. The study presents more learning opportunities than a class can complete in an hour. Select the material that will work best for you. Some groups will want to extend the four-part study to an eight-week course or longer.

It's all about life change. The whole purpose of studying God's Word is to be changed in our character, beliefs, and behavior so that we please God more, become more like Christ, and serve Him more every day.

BIBLE VERSION

The Bible study, as well as the book it is based on, has been prepared using the New King James Version of the Bible. Using that version privately or in class will ensure convenience and clarity, but is not required.

- Any disciple who experienced suffering for His name could "rejoice in that day and leap for joy!"—why? "For indeed your reward is great in heaven" (Luke 6:23).
- Anyone who invited the hungry and needy into their homes could know for certain that they would be blessed—"For you shall

HELPING YOU GET AROUND

You'll see three icons used throughout the study to help you use the material more quickly.

 indicates a key verse, definition, or explanation that you won't want to miss.

 indicates optional material for further study. Use this icon to help you decide what materials you can leave for later.

 *indicates a group process question that focuses on life experience.*

RECOMMENDED RESOURCES

♦ *A Life God Rewards,* by Bruce Wilkinson with David Kopp, is the basis for this study. Reading it first, or in conjunction with the study, will greatly multiply the personal benefits to you.

♦ *A Life God Rewards Devotional* (and accompanying *Journal*), by Bruce Wilkinson with David Kopp, is a thirty-one-day devotional that also follows a four-week structure. On the first day of each week's study, the student is keyed to which chapters in the book and devotional apply to the discussion at hand.

♦ The eight-part *A Life God Rewards* video series, led by the author, will take you to greater depths in each area. Visit www.globalvisionresources.com for more information.

♦ *A Life God Rewards Audio,* read by the author, can provide busy people with an easy way to learn and review the message of the book.

♦ If you are a teenager (or have one in your home), I recommend *A Life God Rewards for Teens,* by Bruce Wilkinson and David Kopp.

♦ For children, see the age-specific *A Life God Rewards* children's books, by Bruce Wilkinson with Mack Thomas, listed in the back of this book.

♦ Visit www.thebreakthroughseries.com for recent updates from Multnomah Publishers authors, new product information, inspiring stories from readers, and other help.

be repaid at the resurrection" (Luke 14:14).

- Every servant who gave money or possessions to God's work on earth could look forward to a lasting return later—"You will have treasure in heaven" (Matthew 19:21).
- And He promised that anyone who gave his life for Christ's sake would actually "find it," because "the Son of Man will come...and then He will reward each according to his works" (Matthew 16:25, 27).

When you begin to see what the New Testament teaches on eternal reward, you'll understand, perhaps for the first time, what the Bible means when it says, "Without faith it is impossible to please Him, *for he who comes to God must believe that...He is a rewarder*" (Hebrews 11:6).

BREAK THROUGH TO ETERNAL REWARD

If you haven't read *A Life God Rewards* yet, I highly recommend that you do so right away. I also encourage you to enhance your learning experience each day for the next month by following along in the *A Life God Rewards Devotional,* the companion *Journal,* and the video series.

By the time you complete this *Life God Rewards Bible Study,* you will see God's tenacious love for you in a new light. You'll better understand His expectations of your life. You'll feel a growing motivation to invest your energies in doing what matters to God. You'll break free from the sins that sabotage your joy now and your potential for even greater joy in heaven.

And you will join millions of others who are living eagerly for the day Jesus promised on the last page of the Bible: "Behold, I am coming quickly, and My reward is with Me, to give to every one according to his work" (Revelation 22:12).

Blessings on your journey!

—Bruce Wilkinson

Week One

THE TRUTH
ABOUT YOUR
ETERNITY

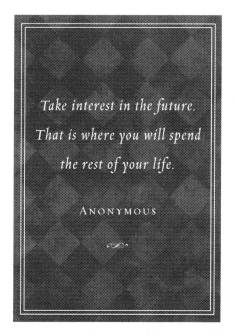

Take interest in the future.
That is where you will spend
the rest of your life.

ANONYMOUS

RECOMMENDED RESOURCES

A Life God Rewards, Chapters 1–2
A Life God Rewards Devotional, Introduction
A Life God Rewards Video Series, Sessions 1–2

GETTING STARTED

I read once that looking at the stars through a telescope on earth is a little like looking up from the bottom of a swimming pool. No matter how powerful the lens, images are unclear. The reason is that a telescope looks up through a deep ocean of atmosphere, so light rays from outer space appear blurred and wobbly.

Now you know why stars appear to twinkle.

And now you know why astronomers were so excited when, in 1990, they launched the Hubble Space Telescope. Hubble studies the stars from an orbit *above* earth's atmosphere. No blur. No wobble. No twinkle. Almost every week, scientists are making new discoveries far out on the edges of time and space.

What if you could see your life like that? What if you could clearly see the results of a choice you make today from a no-wobble viewpoint far out into your future? Think how much it would help you to make the important choices every day brings.

You and I can't see into the future, but Someone can. His name is Jesus. He's not a captive of earth like you and me. Jesus can see the whole truth—past, present, and future—and tell you exactly how to prepare for what is to come.

This chapter has one simple but extremely important purpose: to show you the future Jesus talked about so you know what to do now.

THIS WEEK YOU'LL DISCOVER...

- ♦ the real timeline of your forever life.
- ♦ the two keys that unlock the truth about your eternity.
- ♦ surprising truths about heaven and hell.
- ♦ how your actions today will affect your life in eternity.
- ♦ how knowing the truth about your future can change your life, starting now.

1. WHAT DO I REALLY BELIEVE ABOUT ETERNITY?

1. *How much time do you spend thinking about what will happen in your eternal future? Why do you think this is so?*

YOUR ETERNITY IQ INVENTORY

2. *The following inventory will show what you believe about your eternal future. Score yourself with the numbers 1 through 5 as follows:* Strongly agree. ❷Agree. ❸Unsure. ❹Slightly disagree. ❺Strongly disagree.

___ After I die, the only thing that will matter is whether I accepted Christ as my Savior while I was alive on earth.

___ Once I go to heaven, the big events of my existence will be over.

___ No one can really know what will happen in eternity.

___ It's faith, not works, that will affect my experience of eternity.

___ All of us will experience heaven in the same way.

___ YOUR SCORE: Total the values assigned to the five statements. If you scored…

21–25 WOW! *You're at the top of your class.*

16–20 WHOA! *You've got a passing grade.*

11–15 WISHY-WASHY. *Eternity is a big question mark in the sky for you.*

5–10 WATCH OUT! *You're in for a big shock about how eternity works!*

> **" " TALK POINT " "**
>
> If you could ask God one question about your eternity, what would it be?

3. *How would you live differently if you were absolutely convinced that everything you did in this life had a direct and eternal consequence in the next life?*

2. WHAT WILL HAPPEN IN ETERNITY?

 If we look closely at the Bible and the teachings of Jesus, we can construct an accurate timeline of our eternal existence.

THE SIX MAIN EVENTS OF YOUR ETERNITY

EVENT #1: LIFE. *You are created in the image of God for a life of purpose.* You didn't exist forever in the past, but you will continue to exist forever in the future.

    a. *Read Genesis 1:27–28. What unique identity and responsibility sets a human apart from other life forms?*

    b. *Read 1 Thessalonians 5:23. Between birth and death, you live on earth as* _____ , _____ , *and* _____ .

EVENT #2: DEATH. *You die physically, but not spiritually.* The death of your body is your exit from life on earth. Yet your life as soul and spirit continues.

    Read Hebrews 9:27. Every man will _____ *and this will happen only* _____ .

EVENT #3: DESTINATION. *You reach your eternal destination after death.* Jesus identified only two possible locations in the afterlife: heaven or hell (Matthew 23:33; John 14:2).

    Read John 3:18. Jesus explained clearly how to avoid hell and go to heaven: "He who _____ *in Him is not condemned; but he who does not* _____ *is condemned already, because he has not* _____ *in the name of the only begotten Son of God."*

EVENT #4: RESURRECTION. *You receive a resurrected body.* You will receive a new, immortal body (John 5:28–29; 1 Corinthians 15:51–58).

    Read Philippians 3:20–21. Jesus will transform your earthly _____

    so that it will be conformed to His glorious _____ .

HAVE I BEEN HERE BEFORE?

Around the world, many believe they have lived previous lives as other humans or animals. But neither reincarnation nor "soul sleep" is taught in the Bible. We only die once (Hebrews 9:27). And Jesus revealed that after death our soul is either with God in heaven or apart from God in hell (Matthew 25:41; 2 Corinthians 5:8).

EVENT #5: REPAYMENT. *You receive your eternal reward or your retribution based on what you did on earth.* Everyone's works will be judged by Jesus Christ (John 5:22). They will determine the degree of reward in heaven or retribution in hell (Matthew 23:14; Revelation 20:11–15).

> *Read 2 Corinthians 5:10. For we must all _____ before the judgment seat of Christ, that each one may _____ the things done in the body, according to what he has done, whether _____ or _____.*

EVENT #6: ETERNITY. *You will live forever in the presence or absence of God.* Eternity is a real life in a real place where you will experience the consequences of your beliefs and actions on earth.

> a. *Read Matthew 25:46. Jesus said that those who have rejected Him will experience everlasting _____, while those who have chosen Him will receive eternal _____.*

> b. *Read John 14:1–3. What did Jesus promise His friends in heaven?*

"" TALK POINT ""

Did any of the events described in your timeline surprise you?

If so, why?

How could this information change your life today?

3. WHAT WILL MATTER IN ETERNITY?

1. *Jesus taught that two distinct truths determine everything about our eternity.*

   a. Read John 3:16. Now review Event #3 in your eternal timeline. According to Jesus, what is the key to obtaining eternal life in heaven? _____.

   b. Your answer is the first key:

   ### THE FIRST KEY
   My _____ determines my eternal destination.

2. *The second key is the focus of this Bible study. This key determines not where but how you experience eternity.*

   a. Review Event #5 on your timeline. Now read Matthew 16:27 and fill in the blanks: "The Son of Man (Jesus) will come and then He will reward each according to his _____."

   b. You have identified the second key:

   ### THE SECOND KEY
   My _____ determine my eternal compensation.

3. *Many believers are familiar with the key of belief, or faith. Write out Ephesians 2:8–9 on the lines below:*

   _____

   _____

   _____

   _____

   _____

   _____

" " TALK POINT " "

How do the two keys match up with what you have been taught about faith and works?

4. *Now notice what Ephesians 2:10 says about the key of behavior or works:*

For we are His _____, created in Christ
Jesus for _____ _____, which
God prepared beforehand that we should walk in them.

COMPARING THE TWO KEYS TO MY ETERNITY

CATEGORY	THE FIRST KEY (belief or faith)	THE SECOND KEY (behavior or works)
WHAT I DO	*I believe in Christ*	*I work for Christ*
WHAT I RECEIVE	*A gift from God*	*A reward from God*
WHO DOES THE WORK	*Christ did the work for me*	*I do the work for Christ*
THE BASIS	*My faith in Christ*	*My works for God*
THE RESULT	*My eternal salvation*	*My eternal compensation*

5. *What would be some potential negative consequences if you confused the purpose and promise of the two keys?*

TALK POINT

Why might some
Christians be
suspicious of those
who emphasize
good works?
_____

Why might some
non-Christians
be suspicious of
those who emphasize
only faith?
_____

4. WHAT IS THE SURPRISING TRUTH ABOUT HEAVEN?

KEY Many grow up believing that heaven will be the same experience for everyone—that nothing else you do now could affect your eternity. But the New Testament reveals a different picture.

1. *Read Matthew 16:27. Jesus said that each person will receive something from Him on one basis: "_____ _____ his works."*

2. *Read 2 Corinthians 5:10. Notice again the two words, used by both Paul and Jesus, that indicate varying degrees of reward in heaven: "_____ _____ the things done in the body."*

3. *Read Matthew 19:27–30. What does the reward that Jesus promised the twelve disciples indicate about levels of authority or responsibility in heaven? (See v. 28.)*

" " TALK POINT " "

4. *Read Matthew 25:20–21. Jesus reveals an important principle about how serving Him on earth will be rewarded in heaven. What is it?*

Why is it difficult for many to accept that some will have more reward or authority than others in heaven?

WONDERFUL FOR ALL

e XTRA Although heaven won't be experienced in the same way by everyone, it will be wonderful for all. Look for the universal truths about heaven in these passages: John 14:2–3; 1 John 3:2; Revelation 15:3–4; Revelation 21:2–5.

5. WHAT IS THE SURPRISING TRUTH ABOUT HELL?

KEY Since Jesus reveals that there will be degrees of reward in heaven, you would expect Him also to judge nonbelievers with degrees of punishment.

1. *Read Matthew 11:23–24 and Matthew 23:13–14. What do the words "it shall be more tolerable" and "greater condemnation" suggest about degrees of retribution for wrongdoing?*

2. *Read Romans 2:5–6. How do the words "treasuring up for yourself wrath" point to a connection between the amount of evil committed on earth and the amount of retribution in hell?*

3. *A. W. Tozer wrote, "The vague and tenuous hope that God is too kind to punish the ungodly has become a deadly opiate for the conscience of millions." How might Christians live differently if they accepted the reality of punishment in hell as taught by Jesus?*

Why is the subject of hell so hard for Christians and non-Christians alike?

PROMISES, PROMISES...

Satan promises the best, but pays with the worst:
He promises honor and pays with disgrace;
he promises pleasure and pays with pain;
he promises life and pays with death.

THOMAS BROOKS

THE BEGGAR AND THE RICH MAN
A glimpse behind the curtains of eternity.
[Read Luke 16:19–31]

e XTRA Jesus told a revealing story about two men that shows us a great deal about eternity. The first was a rich man, who enjoyed the best of everything on earth. The other was a beggar named Lazarus, who lived off the crumbs that fell from the rich man's table.

But when the two men died, things changed dramatically. The beggar went to eternal comfort in heaven—in Jesus' story, called "Abraham's bosom." The rich man went to eternal misery in hell.

Now it was the rich man's turn to beg. "Have mercy on me," he cried out to Abraham, trying desperately to strike a deal. Here's a paraphrase of their conversation:

RICH MAN: Father Abraham, have mercy on me! Send Lazarus with a drop of water to cool my tongue, for I am tormented in this flame!

ABRAHAM: Son, it's impossible because there is a great gulf fixed.

RICH MAN: Then I beg you to send Lazarus to earth to talk to my brothers. Otherwise they'll end up in this place of torment too!

ABRAHAM: They don't need anyone, as they already have the Scriptures to tell them the truth.

RICH MAN: Yes, but if someone goes from the dead to talk to my brothers, I know they'll repent!

ABRAHAM: If they won't believe what the Bible says, neither will they believe a witness from the dead.

And with that, the curtains close…

TALK POINT

What does Jesus reveal about God's justice in eternity? (See v. 25.)

Based on Christ's teaching, what would you tell those who say that hell can't be too bad because it will be "one big party with all my friends"?

6. HOW SHOULD I THINK ABOUT ETERNITY TODAY?

If you look at the timeline of eternity (pp. 10–11) in terms of cause and effect, you see that your life on earth—Event #1—determines what happens to you in *every later event* throughout eternity. We can describe this invisible, one-way connection as the Law of the Unbreakable Link.

> ### THE LAW OF THE UNBREAKABLE LINK:
> *Your choices on earth have direct consequences on your life in eternity.*

1. *Picture the Law of the Unbreakable Link as a dot and line. The dot represents your brief life on earth. The endless line represents your life in eternity:*

   • ————————————————➤

   a. *How could this picture change your perspective on choices you will make in the coming week?*

   b. *What two choices during your life on earth will have the most consequences in your eternity? What I _____ and what I _____. (See p. 12.)*

2. *We understand the purpose of positive and negative consequences in our lives as parents/children, teachers/students, and employers/employees. What might be some reasons Jesus revealed the positive consequence of great eternal reward?*

" " TALK POINT " "

Why do you suppose Satan would want people to miss the unbreakable link between today and eternity?

7. WHAT COULD KEEP ME FROM LIVING WITH ETERNITY IN MIND?

After Michelangelo died, someone found in his studio a piece of paper on which he had written a note to his apprentice. It read: "Draw, Antonio, draw, Antonio, draw and do not waste time."

This week we've seen that our work for God will change our eternity. But our opportunity has a time limitation. We are invited to live for God *and not waste time!* (See Ephesians 5:16.)

Take a minute to consider some common reasons people don't live for eternity. Then allow the Word and the Spirit to help you break through to the truth.

1. THE "BIG BLUR" BELIEF. *"I don't think a person can really know what will happen in eternity, and I don't think God expects me to."*

Fact: The Bible is silent on many details of the future, but the facts about events that you are responsible to prepare for are clearly laid out. Just as a parent prepares a child for the "real world" he will someday face, Jesus carefully prepared His followers for their "eternal world."

Response: Read John 14:1–3. Write down two facts about eternity Jesus wanted all His followers to be certain about:

_____

_____

2. THE "NEW TO ME" RESISTANCE. *"I've never heard of this teaching before. How can I trust it to be true?"*

Fact: It is good to carefully evaluate teachings that are new to you. As you've seen, Jesus, Paul, John, James, and Peter all teach eternal rewards. Read what Luther, Calvin, Spurgeon, Wesley, and many others have to say about rewards in the book *A Life God Rewards.*

Response: Read Acts 17:11–12 and describe the actions you should take as you consider eternal rewards:

_____

_____

3. THE "SOCIALISM" STALEMATE. *"I believe that heaven will be the same for everyone. Otherwise, how can it be fair?"*

Fact: It's God's nature and promise to bring perfect justice to the whole world. (Would it be fair for the Christian who lived a compromised, selfish life to experience heaven the same way as someone who sacrificed herself over many years—even to the point of death—for Jesus?) In heaven *and* in hell, not one person will feel unjustly treated. And in heaven, everyone will agree with and rejoice over what God gives to each person.

Response: Read Revelation 11:17–18. This song is a spontaneous testimony from those who have seen God's justice firsthand. Write down truths they reveal about eternity that can renew your mind today:

_____

_____

4. THE "LOVE IS ALL YOU NEED" DEFENSE. *"Jesus came to earth to bring love. And I love God. Isn't that what will matter most in eternity? I think Christianity is about my relationship to Jesus, not my service for Him."*

Fact: Jesus said that loving God and loving others are the greatest commandments. Yet Jesus almost always spoke of love in terms of what we do, not what we feel.

Response: Read Matthew 25:34–40; John 14:21–24; and John 15:9–10. How does Christ link our love for Him and our service for Him?

_____

_____

_____

_____

THE BUSINESS OF NOW

It ought to be the business of every day to prepare for our last day.

MATTHEW HENRY

My Prayer to Live in Light of Eternity

⚬∞⚬

Heavenly Father,
Thank You for creating me for eternity.
Thank You for pursuing me with love, even when I get caught
up in earthly thinking and forget my true destiny in You.
Thank You for sending Your Son, Jesus, to earth to tell us about
heaven and to make a way for every person to join You there.
Please continue to open my eyes to see the invisible
but eternal realities that are so easy to miss.
Change my beliefs and my heart.
I want to see and value my life as You do,
because You are the truth and You can see what I can't.
In Jesus' name, amen.

Now may the God of peace Himself sanctify you completely;
and may your whole spirit, soul,
and body be preserved blameless
at the coming of our Lord Jesus Christ.

1 THESSALONIANS 5:23

Week Two

THE GOOD NEWS
ABOUT REWARDS

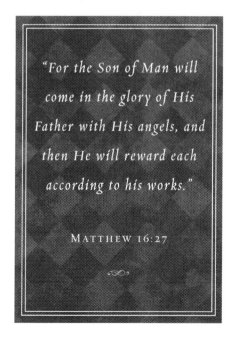

*"For the Son of Man will
come in the glory of His
Father with His angels, and
then He will reward each
according to his works."*

MATTHEW 16:27

RECOMMENDED RESOURCES

A Life God Rewards, Chapter 3
A Life God Rewards Devotional, Week 1
A Life God Rewards Video Series, Sessions 3–4

GETTING STARTED

I remember the day a teenager came to me and told me things didn't add up. "Why should I do what's right if nothing really matters after I'm dead? I'd rather just have fun now."

Have you ever felt that way? If so, this week's study will answer important questions for you. You're going to meet a God who has given you the gift of life for bigger reasons than you imagined. A God who notices, who will make things right, and who will pay you back generously for *everything* you did for Him during your life on earth.

You see, receiving God's gift of salvation and eternal life is just your first step to encountering His amazing love. Jesus came to tell the world that God is our redeemer *and* our rewarder.

Are you willing to think differently about your life and your God? Are you willing to expect more, not less, of God? C. S. Lewis wrote, "If we consider the unblushing promises of reward and the staggering nature of rewards promised in the Gospels, it would seem that our Lord finds our desires not too strong, but too weak."

THIS WEEK YOU'LL DISCOVER...

♦ what Jesus said about eternal reward.
♦ when and how He will reward you.
♦ who else in the Bible lived in light of eternal rewards.
♦ how wrong beliefs might be stealing God's best from you today and in heaven.
♦ how you can break through to a whole new way of thinking.

1. WHAT DO I BELIEVE ABOUT ETERNAL REWARDS?

1. Recall a time when you encouraged someone to do something by offering a reward. Why did you do it? What happened?

MY REWARDS INVENTORY

2. The following inventory will bring to the surface what you believe about eternal rewards. Score yourself with the numbers 1 through 5 as follows: Strongly agree. ❷ Agree. ❸ Unsure. ❹ Slightly disagree. ❺ Strongly disagree.

___ If God wants to reward me for something good I do, He'll bless me for it here on earth, not in heaven.

___ Eternal rewards are for spiritual giants like Billy Graham or Mother Teresa, not ordinary people like me.

___ Eternal rewards are not real and tangible (like money in your pocket); they're just spiritual concepts.

___ Every good thing I do for God is equally lasting and valuable to Him.

___ God already gave the world His Son, so He certainly won't reward me for serving Him!

___ YOUR SCORE: Total the values assigned to the five statements. If you scored…

21–25 GRAND PRIZE.

16–20 GREAT BIG PRIZE.

11–15 PRETTY GOOD PRIZE.

5–10   SORRY, NO PRIZE.

" " TALK POINT " "

How would your life change if you discovered today that you had a millionaire uncle who had guaranteed in writing to reward you with $1,000 for every good deed you did for him for the rest of your life?

2. WHAT DID JESUS REVEAL ABOUT ETERNAL REWARDS?

Jesus chose dramatic occasions to talk about eternal rewards.

1. THE JOYFUL LEAP. *Read Matthew 5:11–12 and Luke 6:22–23. In the Sermon on the Mount, Jesus said His followers are blessed when they suffer persecution for Him because of something that will happen later.*

   a. Where is the reward located? _____.

   b. What emotional response now does Jesus say will come from knowing about His future reward? Fill in the blanks:

   " _____ *and be exceedingly* _____ " *(Matthew 5:12).*

   " _____ *in that day and leap for* _____ !" *(Luke 6:23).*

2. THE SURPRISING DINNER GUEST. *Jesus was invited to dinner at the home of a prominent religious leader. After the guests were seated, Christ gave some startling advice to the host. Read Luke 14:12–14.*

   a. What one word is repeated three times? _____

   b. Did you notice the timing of the repayment? It occurs at the " _____ of the just." How does this insight change how you think about good deeds you've done in the past?

3. THE BOLD QUESTION. *Read Matthew 19:21–30. Jesus had just told a rich young ruler to sell all his belongings and follow Him so he could "have treasure in heaven" (v. 21). The disciples must have overheard. Read verse 27 to see Peter's follow-up question, then read verses 28–30 for Jesus' reply.*

   a. What should Jesus' reply to Peter's question tell us about the *appropriateness* of caring about (and even deeply desiring) reward in heaven?

b. What should His reply tell us about the *potential value* of reward in heaven?

c. How could knowing that God's *greatest* rewards come in heaven (not on earth) help you see the cost of serving God in a new light?

4. THE EXTRAORDINARY EXCHANGE. *Jesus invited His followers to make the most important exchange imaginable—their life now for His reward later. Read Matthew 16:24–27, then write verse 27 on the following lines:*

_____

_____

_____

_____

_____

KEY 5. LET'S SUMMARIZE WHAT WE'VE LEARNED:

a. The rewards Jesus talked about first and foremost don't come on earth but in _____.

b. His rewards are given to "each according to his _____" (Matthew 16:27).

c. The size of the reward in heaven will be _____ (Luke 6:23), even a _____-fold return on our work for God (Matthew 19:29).

d. Knowing about future reward can make us leap for _____ now (Luke 6:23).

" " TALK POINT " "

How does Jesus' emphasis on rewards in heaven match up with what you've been taught about how God blesses, prospers, or rewards His children?

3. WHAT DOES "REWARD" MEAN IN THE BIBLE?

In the New Testament, two Greek words are used most often to describe the rewards God will grant in heaven:

KEY *1. MISTHOS. This Greek word means "wages"—something you earn as a result of something you do. Fill in how misthos is translated in the following examples:*

    a. "Call the laborers and give them their _____, beginning with the last to the first" (Matthew 20:8).

    b. "The laborer is worthy of his _____" (1 Timothy 5:18).

    c. "Indeed the _____ of the laborers who mowed your fields...cry out" (James 5:4).

    d. "Rejoice and be exceedingly glad, for great is your _____ in heaven" (Matthew 5:12).

    e. "But love your enemies, do good, and lend, hoping for nothing in return; and your _____ will be great" (Luke 6:35).

    f. "And behold, I am coming quickly, and My _____ is with Me, to give to every one according to his work" (Revelation 22:12).

2. *Jesus put himself in the role of master or "boss" and described His rewards as "wages." He never described His rewards as a tip or token of appreciation. What is the difference, and why is it significant for those who serve Him?*

"" TALK POINT ""

Why might some resist the idea of God as a "boss" who pays "wages"?

Why might some welcome the idea?

KEY *3.* APODIDOMAI. *The second term used for eternal reward is* apodidomai. *In Greek,* apo *means "back," and* didomai *means "to give." Combined,* apodidomai *means "to give back in return" or simply "repay." Fill in how* apodidomai *is translated in the following examples:*

a. Remember Jesus' story of the Good Samaritan? When the Samaritan took the injured man to a nearby inn for care, he told the innkeeper, "Take care of him; and whatever more you spend, when I come again, I will _____ you" (Luke 10:35).

b. Jesus also used *apodidomai* to describe a person's obligation to pay taxes. He said, "_____ therefore to Caesar the things that are Caesar's, and to God the things that are God's" (Matthew 22:21).

c. "You will be blessed...for you shall be _____ at the resurrection of the just" (Luke 14:14).

d. "Your Father who sees in secret will Himself _____ you openly" (Matthew 6:4).

e. "For the Son of Man will come in the glory of His Father with His angels, and then He will _____ each according to his works" (Matthew 16:27).

DO YOU HAVE TO BELIEVE IN REWARD?

Interestingly, the Bible gives a direct answer to this question. In fact, the writer of Hebrews uses a unique combination of the two Greek words for reward—*misthos-apodidomai*—to describe not just what God will do, but who He is:

> "But without faith it is impossible to please Him, for he who comes to God must believe that He is, and that He is a rewarder [misthos-apodidomai]."
>
> HEBREWS 11:6

If we want to please God, there's no choice. Not only must we believe in the truth of eternal reward, but we must believe in the *Person* of reward—that it is God's very nature to be a rewarder.

4.   WHAT ARE "GOOD WORKS"?

KEY *1. In my book Secrets of the Vine, we saw that good works can be described as fruit—something we do as a Christian to meet a need and bring glory to God. Read in John 15 what Jesus told His friends the night before He died:*

        a. Verse 16—"I chose you and appointed you that you should go and bear _____, and that your _____ should remain."

        b. Verse 8—"By this My Father is glorified, that you bear _____ fruit."

2. *Paul connects fruit directly to good works in Titus 3:14—"Let our people also learn to maintain _____ _____, to meet urgent needs, that they may not be _____."*

3. *Take another look at Ephesians 2:10—"For we are His workmanship, created in Christ Jesus for _____ _____, which God prepared beforehand that we should walk in them."*

4. *Is the idea that you have been "created" for good works new to you? How might knowing this help you distinguish between works you are called to do and works that someone else might be called to do? On the lines below, list at least three good works you enjoy doing for God:*

_____

_____

_____

_____

_____

_____

" " TALK POINT " "

Can you think of some activities Christians might do that may seem spiritual, but aren't necessarily "good works" God would reward?

5. WHAT SPECIFIC WORKS WILL GOD REWARD?

1. *Some passages link good works directly with a reward. Complete the chart below by looking up the Scriptures and filling in the boxes.*

SCRIPTURES	What Present Behavior IS COMMANDED?	What Future Result IS PROMISED?
I TIMOTHY 6:18–19	*Do good works, be ready to give, willing to share*	
COLOSSIANS 3:23–24	*Serve your master "as to the Lord"*	
LUKE 6:35		*Reward will be great*
MATTHEW 6:3–4	*Charitable deeds*	
MATTHEW 6:6		*Reward openly*
MATTHEW 6:17–18	*Fast in private*	

è XTRA

2. Jesus describes six acts of service He will reward when He returns (Matthew 25:31–40). What are they? (See vv. 35–36.)

a. "I was _____ and you _____."

b. "I was _____ and you _____."

c. "I was _____ and you _____."

d. "I was _____ and you _____."

e. "I was _____ and you _____."

f. "I was _____ and you _____."

" " TALK POINT " "

Jesus said when we serve "the least of these," we are actually serving Him (Matthew 25:40). How could knowing this change how you respond to needs around you?

6. WHO ARE SOME BIBLE PEOPLE THAT LIVED FOR REWARD?

MOSES, PRINCE OF EGYPT:

The man who "looked to the reward."

[Read Hebrews 11:23–29]

Moses was raised as an adopted son in Pharaoh's household during a time when other Israelites were being mistreated as slaves in Egypt. But in an act of faith, he chose to lead God's people out of slavery and to the Promised Land. (For background reading, see Acts 7:20–36.)

1. *The writer of Hebrews shows the powerful role of faith in Moses' life. Fill in the blanks: Moses esteemed "the reproach of Christ greater riches than the treasures in Egypt; for he* _____ ____ _____ _____ *" (Hebrews 11:26).*

2. *During his years of leading the Israelites through the wilderness, Moses faced nearly every kind of physical and emotional challenge. Would you say Moses believed that the reward he looked for was [check one]:*

   __ highly desirable, but not guaranteed?

   __ guaranteed, but not as real as Pharaoh's treasure?

   __ real, guaranteed, *and* highly desirable?

PAUL, WITNESS TO KINGS:

The man who ran for the prize.

[Read 1 Corinthians 9:24–27; 2 Corinthians 5:9–11]

Paul was a zealous Pharisee until a dramatic conversion experience brought him to Christ (Acts 9:3–9). Paul became known as the Apostle to the Gentiles, witnessing before kings and governors. Near the end of his life, he wrote, "For to me, to live is Christ, and to die is gain" (Philippians 1:21).

"" TALK POINT ""

Think of a time in your life when knowing an earthly reward was coming made it easier for you to endure a difficult task. How could Paul's example encourage you to persevere in a difficult spiritual challenge?

1. In 1 Corinthians 9:24–27, Paul gives a memorable picture of the life of faith. He uses the metaphor of an athletic contest.

    a. How does he advise Christians to run their race? (See vv. 24–25.)

    b. What reward does he say Christians are running to win? (See v. 25.)

2. Paul gives personal insight into how living for reward changed his life:

    a. He ran "not with _____ " (v. 26).

    b. He applied physical _____ to his body (v. 27).

3. The context of these remarks is works, not salvation. What negative result did Paul want to avoid at all costs in his personal race of faith? (See v. 27.)

4. List three words that describe how you have been running your race of faith recently: _____ _____ _____

AND DON'T FORGET JOHN

JOHN BUNYAN—"Whatever good thing you do for Him, if done according to the Word, is laid up for you as treasure in chests and coffers, to be brought out to be rewarded before both men and angels, to your eternal comfort."

JOHN CALVIN—"It is my happiness that I have served Him who never fails to reward His servants to the full extent of His promise."

THE APOSTLE JOHN—"Look to yourselves, that we do not lose those things we worked for, but that we may receive a full reward" (2 John 1:8).

7. WHAT IS KEEPING ME FROM WANTING ETERNAL REWARD?

Most who learn about eternal reward for the first time are eager to act on what they've discovered, and their lives begin to change immediately. Others respond cautiously, or even with resistance. One person told me, "But I was happy serving God because I love Him. I don't need or want reward!" Another said, "I feel unspiritual every time you say the word *reward!*"

Can you relate to these feelings? If so, be encouraged. The fact that you're struggling to come to grips with Christ's teachings says good things about you. You want to do the right thing for the right reasons. You care about genuineness and integrity in your relationship with God.

In the list below, check any attitudes or beliefs you recognize that might be keeping you from wanting the rewards Jesus talked about. Then take a few minutes to respond to the teaching that follows.

1. THE "SELFISH" UNCERTAINTY. *"Wanting a reward for serving God sounds selfish. How can that honor God?"*

Fact: Any act is selfish only if you put yourself before others, or prevent others from receiving a share of what you have. (For example, you eat the last piece of cheesecake knowing that your spouse wanted it too.) But God rewards each of us personally and out of His limitless bounty. When you receive a reward from Him, no one else is losing what would rightfully be theirs.

Response: Write out your new belief:

Wanting eternal reward from God is not selfish because _____

_____

_____

_____

2. THE "UNWORTHY SERVANT" STANCE. *"But God has already done so much for me. I don't deserve a reward!"*

Fact: You're right. We're unworthy servants, working for God because of our love for Him. But God's plan to reward, like His plan to redeem, is not based on our merit but on His grace. We may be unworthy, but God is generous beyond measure!

Response: Read Luke 17:10 and James 1:17. Write out your new belief:

Even though I don't deserve any reward from God, I will accept His generosity and highly value His reward because _____

_____

_____

_____

3. THE "MOTIVATION SITUATION" MIX-UP. *"I feel unspiritual when you talk about being rewarded. I want to keep my motives pure."*

Fact: To be motivated by reward is pleasing to God. He created us as complex beings who choose how to act for many reasons. Too often people confuse the idea of mixed motives with multiple motives. *Mixed motives* means that both good intentions and bad intentions are causing our behavior. But *multiple motives* simply means we're doing something for more than one good reason. You already work for God because you love Him, because you want to obey, and because you love others. Adding God's reward to the mix is a godly thing to do.

Would God tell you that He is a rewarder, then get upset at you if you thought of Him that way? That wouldn't make sense. Acknowledging a desire for eternal reward isn't succumbing to temptation because any motivation from God is pure, and it is impossible for God to tempt us.

Response: Read 2 Corinthians 5:9–10; Hebrews 11:6; and James 1:13, 17. Write out your new belief:

To strongly desire to receive God's approval and reward in heaven, and to order my life accordingly, is pleasing to Him because _____

_____

_____

_____

My Prayer to Live

for God's Reward

⸎

Dear Lord,
I praise and thank You for Your grace and goodness.
I believe Your promise that You will reward Your servant
"each according to his works."
Forgive me for doubting Your generosity.
Forgive me for accepting Your gift of salvation without taking
up my opportunity to do Your work on earth.
Help me to order my life in such a way that I please You,
serve You, and honor You in all I do.
And may the fruit of my brief time on earth bring
You joy for all eternity.
Amen.

"And behold, I am coming quickly,
and My reward is with Me,
to give to every one according to his work."
REVELATION 22:12

Week Three

THE GOOD NEWS
OF THE BEMA

> "We make it our aim...to be
> well pleasing to Him. For
> we must all appear before
> the judgment seat of Christ,
> that each one may receive
> the things done in the body,
> according to what he has
> done, whether good or bad."
>
> 2 CORINTHIANS 5:9–10

RECOMMENDED RESOURCES

A Life God Rewards, Chapter 4
A Life God Rewards Devotional, Week 2
A Life God Rewards Video Series, Sessions 5–6

GETTING STARTED

The last book of the Old Testament depicts a group of believers who saw how much the wicked were prospering and began to doubt that God still cared for those who served Him. They said:

> *"It is useless to serve God;*
> *What profit is it that we have kept His ordinance?"*
>
> MALACHI 3:14

Have you ever felt that way? If so, you're going to enjoy this week's study. You're going to learn more about God's amazing plan to bring justice in eternity and reward His people for everything they do for Him on earth. We'll use as our key texts the teachings of Jesus and Paul on "that Day"—a time when each of us will give an account of our lives to God and receive His justice and generosity.

THIS WEEK YOU'LL DISCOVER...

♦ a God who is more fair than you thought.
♦ what happens at the bema in heaven.
♦ why accountability is good news for every follower of Jesus.
♦ how wrong beliefs can rob you of God's best for you in eternity.
♦ how to live with the bema in mind, starting now.

1. WHAT DO I BELIEVE ABOUT GOD'S JUDGMENT?

1. *Have you ever stood before a judge? Why? What happened? What are some of the feelings you remember from that event?*

MY ACCOUNTABILITY INVENTORY
What do I believe about judgment after death?

2. *The following inventory will bring to the surface what you believe about God's justice and your accountability. Score yourself as follows:* ❶ Strongly agree. ❷ Agree. ❸ Unsure. ❹ Slightly disagree. ❺ Strongly disagree.

___ Only nonbelievers will have their earthly works judged after death.

___ As a Christian, my sins are forgiven, so how I lived on earth won't come up in heaven.

___ How I worked for God won't matter in eternity, only how much.

___ God loves me too much to judge my works for Him.

___ Earthly injustices, unfairness, and suffering will be overlooked by God in eternity.

___ YOUR SCORE: Total the values assigned to the five statements. If you scored…

21–25 YOUR CASE IS SOLID.

16–20 YOU COULD LOSE ON APPEAL.

11–15 TIME TO TAKE A RECESS.

5–10 DID YOU HEAR THAT GAVEL?

" " TALK POINT " "

What if you knew that from this moment on, everything you ever did would be caught on film—to be reviewed one day by the person you love and respect the most? How would your life change?

2. WILL CHRISTIANS BE ACCOUNTABLE IN ETERNITY?

KEY 1. *Many Christians believe that since their sins are forgiven, they will not have to give an account in heaven for what they did for God while they were on earth. But that is not what the Bible teaches. On earth we have the opportunity to accept or reject Jesus as our Savior. But in heaven, we will meet Him in a different role.*

a. Read Romans 14:10–12. Who will judge you in eternity? _____. (See also John 5:22; Acts 10:42; 2 Timothy 4:1, 8.)

b. What percentage of Christians will stand before the judgment seat of Christ? _____. (See Romans 14:10, 12.)

c. Romans 14:12 reveals what we will give to Jesus at that time. What is it? _____.

d. If you are a Christian, your Judge is also your Savior and High Priest. Read Hebrews 2:17–18 and Hebrews 4:14–16. List some things about Jesus that uniquely qualify Him to be our righteous judge.

PASSING JUDGMENT ON "JUDGMENT"

If the word *judgment* leaves you feeling nervous or guilty, you might be missing the promise of God's goodness. To judge means to make a decision. A righteous judge measures every decision by what is right and fair. His verdict brings justice to a person or situation. That's why all through Scripture, God's people expressed a desire for, and trust in, God's judgments. David wrote:

> *The trees of the woods shall rejoice before the LORD,*
> *For He is coming to judge the earth.*
> *Oh, give thanks to the LORD, for He is good!*
> *For His mercy endures forever.*

I CHRONICLES 16:33–34

WHAT PAUL TAUGHT ABOUT JUDGMENT

One day Paul was brought before a magistrate in Corinth and accused of persuading people to "worship God contrary to the law" (Acts 18:13). The judge sat on a platform called a bema (pronounced BEE-muh). The magistrate decided that Paul had not broken the law, but Paul's experience in Corinth adds special meaning to what he wrote about another bema—the bema of Christ:

> *For we must all appear before the judgment seat [bema] of Christ, that each one may receive the things done in the body, according to what he has done, whether good or bad.*
>
> 2 CORINTHIANS 5:10

KEY *2. In New Testament times, the bema (which means "judgment seat" in Greek) represented justice and authority. Officials at athletic contests also sat on a bema to determine winners and distribute awards. Reread 2 Corinthians 5:10 and fill in the blanks:*

a. "We must all appear" shows that _____ , not just some, will be judged.

b. The Person sitting on the bema of heaven will be _____ .

c. "Each one" shows that we will be judged not as a group but as _____ .

d. "Things done in the body" shows that rewards will be based on deeds we did while we were _____ on earth.

e. "May receive" and "according to what he has done" indicate that a reward may or may _____ be given at that time.

" " TALK POINT " "

Is the news of the bema new to you?

Why do you think some Christians aren't aware of the judgment seat of Christ even though the Bible discusses it repeatedly?

3. WHAT WILL HAPPEN AT THE BEMA?

KEY

1. *In 1 Corinthians 3:12–14, Paul describes what will happen at the bema of Jesus. He uses the image of a building (representing your life) that rests on a foundation (Jesus). Consider what these verses tell us about what will happen at the bema:*

a. "Each one's work will become _____; for the Day will _____ it, because it will be _____ ____ _____."

b. "The fire will _____ each one's _____, of what sort it is."

c. "Gold, silver, [and] precious stones" would represent what kinds of works?

d. "Wood, hay, [and] straw" would represent what kinds of works?

e. If a person's work for God endures the fire at the bema, "he will receive a _____."

2. *Paul eagerly anticipated his appearance before Jesus. Read 2 Timothy 4:6–8.*

a. What reward did Paul especially anticipate receiving?

b. Which followers of Jesus can look forward to the same reward?

" " TALK POINT " "

Try to identify three things you did for God recently that you believe would fall in the "gold, silver, [and] precious stones" category. What could you do to make those actions a larger part of your life?

A LIFE REVEALED BY FIRE

The story of Amy Carmichael, missionary to India.

è XTRA Amy Carmichael served God by caring for discarded and abused girls in southern India. Most of them had been abandoned or sold into slavery as temple child prostitutes. Although she was a pale-skinned young Irishwoman, Miss Carmichael dressed in Indian garb, learned the local language, and didn't leave India for fifty-seven years.

What motivated such an amazing life of ministry? Amy Carmichael's biographer, Elisabeth Elliot, traces her inspiring life to a turning point when Amy was a young girl in Belfast....

One rainy Sunday, Amy was walking home from church in her best clothes when she and her two brothers met a ragged old woman carrying a heavy load. Deciding they should help, they took the woman's load and guided her through the streets.

"This meant facing all the respectable people who were, like ourselves, on their way home," Amy recalled later. "It was a horrid moment. We were only two boys and a girl, and not at all exalted Christians. We hated doing it."

As they passed a fountain, a Scripture flashed into Amy's mind:

...gold, silver, precious stones, wood, hay, straw, each one's work will become clear; for the Day will declare it, because it will be revealed by fire; and the fire will test each one's work, of what sort it is. If anyone's work which he has built on it endures, he will receive a reward. (1 Corinthians 3:12–14)

Amy turned, certain that someone had spoken the familiar Scripture to her. But she saw no one—only the fountain, and the falling rain, and people staring at their little procession.

"The children plodded on," Elliot writes, "but something had happened to the girl which changed forever her life's values." A life "revealed by fire" became the measure of what was worth doing for Amy Carmichael. And her work and example continue to change lives for God around the world.

ADAPTED FROM *A Life God Rewards Devotional*

4. HOW CAN I "SUFFER LOSS" AT THE BEMA?

The tested-by-fire passage ends with these words: "If anyone's work is burned, he will suffer loss; but he himself will be saved, yet so as through fire" (1 Corinthians 3:15). Obviously, some things will burn up at the bema.

WHAT IS *not* TESTED AT THE BEMA?

KEY To fully understand what will be tested at the bema of Jesus, we should be very clear on what will *not* be up for review there.

1. YOU *will not be tested. Notice that the emphasis in all these passages is not on who you are, but on what you _____. You will not be subjected to fire, only your _____.*

2. YOUR BELIEFS *will not be tested, and you cannot lose your salvation at the bema. Read John 5:24 and 6:27. Jesus reveals that the person who believes in Him "_____ _____ life." Therefore, the purpose of the judgment seat of Christ cannot be to review your eternal destination.*

3. YOUR SINS *will not be judged. To stand at the bema, you must already be in heaven, forgiven of your sins because of what you believed about Jesus while you were alive on earth. Because you put your faith in Him for your salvation, God accepted His death on Calvary as full, once-and-for-all payment for your sins. You can never again be judged for them.*

Read Hebrews 10:12, 14, 17.

a. "For by one offering He has _____ _____ those who are being sanctified" (v. 14).

b. "Their sins and their lawless deeds I will remember _____ _____ " (v. 17).

" " TALK POINT " "

How does it make you feel to know that when you stand before Jesus, He won't revisit your sins?

LOSS IN HEAVEN

If our salvation won't be tested at the bema and our sins won't be revisited, how could we "suffer loss"? In last week's study, we saw that even the apostle Paul disciplined himself so that he would not "become disqualified" (1 Corinthians 9:27). Paul did not fear losing his *salvation* (which is a gift), but the Lord's *commendation* (which is a reward).

KEY Second John 1:8 says, "Look to yourselves, that we do not lose those things we worked for, but that we may receive a full reward." Clearly, then, a Christian may through wrong choices miss out on his "full reward."

1. *How could major sin in a person's life prevent him or her from receiving a "full reward" in heaven?*

2. *Think of one area where you most want to receive God's "Well done!" when you get to heaven:*

   _____.

3. *List three practical ways in which you could guard or redirect your choices this week so that you won't "suffer loss":*

   a. _____.

   b. _____.

   c. _____.

" " TALK POINT " "

Can you recall a time when a Christian you admired fell into major sin and created spiritual harm to you or others?

What were some of the consequences?

CONFIDENT AND NOT ASHAMED

And now, little children, abide in Him, that when He appears, we may have confidence and not be ashamed before Him at His coming.

1 JOHN 2:28

5. WHAT WILL ENDURE THE FIRE AT THE BEMA?

Jesus told His followers they had been chosen to bear fruit that would "remain" (John 15:16). Consider these criteria for enduring quality in what you do for God today:

1. *Enduring works are done in God's love.*

   a. Read Luke 6:35. If we love our enemies, "hoping for nothing in return," our reward will be _____.

   b. According to 1 Corinthians 13:3, how much "profit" comes from a good work done without love? _____

2. *Enduring works are done in God's power.*

   a. Jesus said, "He who abides in Me, and I in him, bears much fruit; for without Me you can do _____" (John 15:5).

   b. Read Acts 1:8 and 2 Peter 1:2–3. Where does the power to live for God come from? _____.

3. *Enduring works are done for God's glory.*

   a. Read Matthew 6:1–6, 16–18. How much eternal reward comes from "religious" activities that are motivated by personal ego? _____.

   b. How should we pray, give, and fast? _____.

4. *Enduring works are done according to God's will.*

   a. Jesus said, "I do not seek My own will but the _____ of the _____ who sent Me" (John 5:30).

   b. What is a major reason we don't do God's will? (See Philippians 2:20–21.) _____.

> **TALK POINT**
>
> A life God rewards is not about a performance apart from a living relationship with Jesus. How might greater intimacy with God result naturally in greater service to Him?

6. HOW WILL GOD REWARD ME FOR WORKS THAT ENDURE?

1. *Next week, we'll see that the rewards Jesus will distribute at the bema will have a significant and lasting impact on how we experience heaven. The Bible doesn't give an exhaustive list of rewards, but several are mentioned.*

   a. Jesus told the twelve disciples they would "sit on twelve thrones, _____ the twelve tribes of Israel" (Matthew 19:28).

   b. Jesus told all His followers, "If anyone serves Me, him My Father will _____" (John 12:26).

2. *The Greek word for a believer's crown is* stephanos *(denoting a laurel wreath presented to winners at athletic events).*

   a. Read 1 Peter 5:1–4. Church leaders who care for "the flock of God" will receive the crown of _____.

   b. Read James 1:12 and Revelation 2:10. Those who endure severe temptations and suffering will receive a _____ of _____. (This doesn't refer to the gift of eternal life but a special reward for good works.)

   c. Read 2 Timothy 4:6–8. Those who live with the Lord's return in mind will receive a _____ of _____.

   d. Read 1 Thessalonians 2:19 and Daniel 12:3. Those who bring others to God may receive a "crown of _____."

"WILL I GIVE MY CROWNS BACK TO JESUS?"

We often sing or say that we'll worship Jesus in heaven by casting our crowns at His feet. This popular assumption is based on Revelation 4:10–11. Yet these verses do not refer to all believers, but describe a specific group of elders who are performing an act of worship that they will repeat throughout eternity.

Will we long to worship God? Absolutely! And we will do so joyfully and freely forever. But the rewards of Jesus to His followers will be ours *eternally*.

7. WHAT'S KEEPING ME FROM LIVING FOR THE DAY WHEN I STAND BEFORE JESUS?

Do you remember the discouraged believers we met in Malachi (page 36)? I want you to know how God responded to them. The Bible records:

> *The LORD listened and heard them;*
> *So a book of remembrance was written before Him*
> *For those who fear the LORD*
> *And who meditate on His name.*
>
> MALACHI 3:16

God not only cares about His servants, but He wants us to know that He is keeping a "book of remembrance" of everything we do for Him. Not that He has a bad memory! It's us who are often in danger of forgetting that everything we do for God will matter forever.

Do you trust God to care about your work for Him today?

If you recognize yourself in any of the statements on the following page, take a few minutes to let God's Word change your thinking. Then write out your new breakthrough belief.

THEIR DEEDS WILL FOLLOW THEM

Then I heard a voice from heaven saying to me, "Write: Blessed are the dead who die in the Lord from now on." "Yes," says the Spirit, "they will rest from their labor, for their deeds will follow them."

REVELATION 14:13, NIV

SAY WHAT?

❑ <u>WHAT JUSTICE?</u> *I used to doubt that God would make everything right and fair eventually, bringing all people to accountability and justice in eternity.*
    Read Psalm 56:8; Matthew 11:21–22; Romans 2:5–6.
    Now I believe...

❑ <u>WHAT RESULTS?</u> *I used to believe that God wasn't interested in the results of my life as long as my beliefs were biblical.*
    Read Jeremiah 17:10; Luke 19:11–27; Ephesians 2:8–10; Titus 3:14.
    Now I believe...

❑ <u>WHAT GOOD WORKS?</u> *I used to believe that since I was saved by grace, none of my good works would make a difference to me in heaven.*
    Read Matthew 5:1–12; 2 Corinthians 5:9–10; 2 Peter 1:2–11.
    Now I believe...

❑ <u>WHAT JUDGMENT?</u> *I used to think that, since I was saved, I would not be judged by Christ for what I did with my life.*
    Read Matthew 16:27; Luke 12:2; John 5:22–27; 2 Corinthians 4:16–5:11; Hebrews 4:13.
    Now I believe...

❑ <u>WHAT LOSS IN HEAVEN?</u> *I used to believe that once I got to heaven, I would never "suffer loss" of any kind, even if I had let sin and disobedience take away the opportunities to serve God in my life on earth.*
    Read Luke 19:20–26; 1 Corinthians 3:13–15; 2 John 1:8.
    Now I believe...

My Prayer to Live for "That Day"

Dear Lord,
You have shown me that I have an appointment to stand before
You—my God and Friend and Savior—
to give an account of what I did for You on earth.
Oh, may that be the best day of my life!
May it be a day when I see great joy on Your face,
and hear You say, "Well done, good and faithful servant!"
I want to live in such a way that I can eagerly look forward to
that day. Help me not to waste time. Show me how to invest
only in what will endure the fire at the bema. May I never lose
the reward You want so much to give. Thank You that I can
completely trust in Your goodness, fairness, generosity, and love.
Amen.

*I pray that you...may be filled to the
measure of all the fullness of God.
Now to him who is able to do immeasurably more
than all we ask or imagine, according to his power
that is at work within us, to him be glory!*

EPHESIANS 3:17, 19–21, NIV

Week Four

LIVING FOR GOD'S "WELL DONE!"

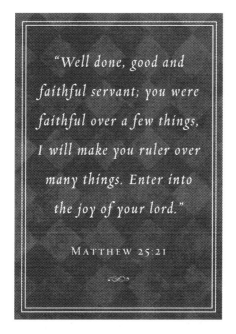

"Well done, good and faithful servant; you were faithful over a few things, I will make you ruler over many things. Enter into the joy of your lord."

MATTHEW 25:21

RECOMMENDED RESOURCES

A Life God Rewards, Chapters 5–6, 8
A Life God Rewards Devotional, Week 3
A Life God Rewards Video Series, Sessions 7–8

GETTING STARTED

"How do you make a thousand dollars when all you have in your pocket is a dime?"

I remember posing the question to my wife. We were starting a family and trying to get by on my salary as a first-year college professor.

But a few days later, things began to change. I spotted a run-down house for sale that I thought I could fix up for a profit. So I used the dime to call my father. Dad agreed to loan me $3,000 for a down payment.

After I bought the house and started renovating, I discovered that I didn't have enough time to both remodel and teach. So I made a deal with a builder friend—he would provide the skilled labor, I would buy the materials, and we would split the profit.

Three months later, we sold the renovated house. After dividing the earnings with my partners, I still took home $14,000—more money than my entire year's salary! My investment of one dime had yielded a huge return.

This week's study is about investing what God has given you now—your time, talents, and treasure—for great and lasting reward in eternity. Actually, you're going to see that working toward a huge return on the investment of your life is not just a good option, it's what Jesus expects from every one of His followers.

THIS WEEK YOU'LL DISCOVER...

- ♦ what God desires and expects from your opportunities today.
- ♦ how what you do with your time, talents, and treasure can change your eternity.
- ♦ the truth about treasure in heaven: Is it real? valuable?
- ♦ how you can "lay up" treasure in heaven.
- ♦ how you can break through to a life God will greatly reward.

1. WHAT DO I THINK MY LIFE IS WORTH?

1. What do you think of when you hear the word stewardship?

MY STEWARDSHIP INVENTORY

2. The following inventory will bring to the surface what you believe about your work for God. Score yourself with the numbers 1 through 5 as follows: **①**Strongly disagree. **❷**Slightly disagree. **❸**Unsure. **❹**Agree. **❺**Strongly agree.

___ My Master evaluates my work for Him by results, not only by effort or good intentions.

___ When I fail to wisely invest my time and talents, I forfeit future opportunities to serve God in heaven.

___ God's rewards for me will be in direct proportion to how I multiplied my resources for His kingdom.

___ I am responsible now to lay up treasure for myself in heaven.

___ In heaven, treasure will be real, valuable, and highly desired.

___ YOUR SCORE: Total the values assigned to the five statements. If you scored…

21–25 WELL DONE!

16–20 GOOD JOB.

11–15 HMM…

5–10 YOU WHAT?

3. Have you or someone you know invested money—only to lose, instead of gain? What happened next?

If you think of your life in terms of assets, what are some of God's greatest investments in your life?

2. WHAT SHOULD I DO WITH MY TIME AND TALENTS?

Jesus told stories about servants and stewards for an important reason.

PORTRAIT OF A STEWARD
[Read Luke 19:11–27, the Parable of the Minas.]

KEY *In this parable, a nobleman entrusts each of his servants with a mina (about three years' wages) and says, "Do business till I come." Then he leaves on a long journey. When he returns, he asks his servants for an account. Based on their results, he distributes (or withholds) reward. Notice the portrait of a steward's life in the parable:*

Begin - ➤ End				
The Commission of the Steward	The Master Leaves	The Opportunity of the Steward	The Master Returns	The Reward of the Steward

1. *Look at the chart of a steward's life. Which box describes the period of time when the steward can make the greatest impact on his future?*

2. *What vital information about their future did this parable tell the twelve disciples?*

3. *The parable also describes our life as God's servants today. For example:*
   What is our *commission?* (Matthew 28:18–20)

   _____

   _____ .

   What is our *opportunity?* (Matthew 19:27–29; John 12:26; Galatians 6:9)

   _____

   _____ .

" " TALK POINT " "

Recall a time when you were put in charge of someone else's home, valuables, or child while they were away. How seriously did you take that commitment?

Three Servants, Three Stories
The truth about our work and God's reward.

The minas represent all that God entrusts us with, not just money. In the Parable of the Minas, Jesus shows how God will respond in eternity to how well we stewarded our opportunities for Him on earth.

1. *The First Servant's Story*
   a. He multiplied _____ mina to _____ minas (v. 16).
   b. His praise from the master: "Well done, _____ _____" (v. 17).
   c. His reward: "Because you were faithful in a very _____, have authority over _____ cities" (v. 17).

2. *The Second Servant's Story*
   a. He multiplied _____ mina to _____ minas (v. 18).
   b. His reward: "You also be over _____ cities" (v. 19).
   c. What words of praise were missing? _____ _____ _____ _____."

3. *The Third Servant's Story*
   a. He started with _____ mina and ended with _____ mina (v. 20).
   b. Not only was praise missing, but the master described him as a "_____ servant" (v. 22).
   c. Instead of reward, the master said, "____ the mina from him" (v. 24).

4. *This story reveals four important insights for all who serve God.*
   a. The assets entrusted to us are actually owned by _____, not us.
   b. God wants us to take what He's entrusted us with and greatly _____ it for His kingdom.
   c. Our future _____ will be directly proportionate to how much we have multiplied what He's given us now.
   d. If we don't invest what God has given us on earth, we will "suffer _____" in heaven. (See 1 Corinthians 3:15.)

Now and Then

Earth for work, heaven for wages—this life for the battle, another for the crown—time for employment, eternity for enjoyment.

3. HOW MUCH DOES GOD EXPECT FROM MY LIFE?

God wants and expects an extraordinary future for all of us—a life of *great return* for Him now, and an eternity of *great reward* from Him later.

1. *Interestingly, when people first study the Parable of the Minas, they often rush to defend the unproductive servant. "Wasn't he just being careful with what he had?" they ask. "Besides, he didn't steal or lose anything." Yet clearly, the third servant did not produce at the level his master expected when he said, "Do business till I come."*

   The master clearly expected to realize [check one]:

❏ Huge returns	❏ Some returns	❏ Little or no return

   The third servant produced as if his master expected [check one]:

❏ Huge returns	❏ Some returns	❏ Little or no return

2. *Read Matthew 28:19–20. Jesus Christ clearly revealed for His disciples and all His future followers what He expected from their lives. Imagine that the third servant lives today on an island in the Atlantic. Write out how he might restate the great commission in terms of what he actually plans to do for God:*

   _____

   _____

   _____

   _____

   _____

   _____

   _____

   _____

   _____

"" TALK POINT ""

How accurately do you think the third servant's behavior illustrates how some Christians live?

Does the truth that God wants much fruit from your life—and cares deeply about results—surprise you?

If so, why?

DIFFERENT ABILITY, EQUAL OPPORTUNITY
[Read Matthew 25:14–30, the Parable of the Talents.]

KEY 3. *You may be thinking, But I don't have many talents or opportunities. How can I realize much return for my life? Jesus brought encouraging news in another parable about servants. This parable follows the same pattern as the Parable of the Minas. But this time, three stewards are each given different amounts of money—"to each according to his own ability" (v. 15).*

   a. Two servants double what they were given. Even though they start—and end—with different amounts, they receive the _____ praise and _____ reward (vv. 15–23).

   b. As in the mina parable, the third servant neglects his commission and does nothing. What happens to his talent? (v. 28)

4. *In this parable, Jesus reveals a principle of potential: The degree of our _____ in heaven will be based on our total results in light of our _____ (what each of us was capable of doing with what we have).*

5. *Read Luke 12:48. What should you say to a friend who habitually envies others who seem more talented, attractive, or blessed?*

THE FIRST CHURCH: A CASE STUDY IN EXPONENTIAL GROWTH

e XTRA When Jesus gave His disciples their "opportunity" as stewards, He asked them to do nothing short of reach the entire globe with His message (Matthew 28:19–20). But how could a handful of ordinary people accomplish such an outrageous goal? It would take *exponential* growth—human dedication and effort multiplied by the power of the Holy Spirit. To see what happened, read Acts 1:8; 2:38–47; and 6:1–7. What practical lessons do these verses suggest about how *you* can accomplish great things for God today?

4. WHAT SHOULD I DO WITH MY TREASURE?

Jesus spoke often about money and belongings. Circle true or false below to show what you think most Christians think they're supposed to believe:

TRUE OR FALSE: You're more spiritual if you don't want treasure.

TRUE OR FALSE: You shouldn't store up treasure for yourself.

TRUE OR FALSE: You won't think about treasure in heaven.

TRUE OR FALSE: Treasure in heaven isn't real.

The answer for each is *false*. What did Jesus *really* say about treasure?

KEY *1. Read Matthew 6:19–24. Jesus gave us specific advice about what to do—and what not to do—with our treasures.*

a. In verse 19, Jesus defines earthly treasure as being something valuable that's subject to _____, _____ or _____.

b. List three things you own that Jesus would call treasure: _____, _____, and _____.

c. What are we not to do with this kind of treasure? "Do _____ lay up for yourselves _____ on _____" (v. 19).

2. *Now read verse 20.*

a. Jesus is giving a command in this passage. What are we supposed to do? "But _____ _____ treasure."

b. For whom? "For _____."

c. Where? "In _____."

3. *Jesus doesn't want to take away our treasure; He wants to help us keep it forever in heaven. How might this fact change the way you respond when your pastor encourages you to give?*

" " TALK POINT " "

Jesus never revealed how treasure will be measured in heaven, or what it will look like. But He clearly taught that it will still be *real* treasure— highly desirable and valuable. How does this fit with what you have believed in the past?

5. HOW DO I MOVE MY TREASURE FROM EARTH TO HEAVEN?

1. One day Jesus told a wealthy young man how to have treasure in heaven. Read Matthew 19:21. What was his advice?

2. *Jesus repeated the same principle—give treasure away to God's work here to receive treasure from God in heaven—in Luke 12:33. As a follower of Jesus you should _____ what you have and _____ alms. This will provide you with _____ in heaven that will not _____.*

3. *Read 1 Timothy 6:17–19. This passage repeats the idea that we must give here to lay up treasure in heaven. How does it indicate that treasure in heaven will have an important purpose?*

4. *Read Luke 21:1–4, the story of the widow's mite. Clearly, what matters most is how much you give of what you have—not the amount you give. With this in mind, how would you rate your giving?*

❏ A little given of a lot owned	❏ Some given of quite a lot owned	❏ Quite a lot given of not much owned	❏ A lot given of a little owned

5. *If we must give away treasure here to God's purposes in order to have it in heaven, how might that change who or what you give to?*

HOW MUCH?

We ask how much a man gives;
Christ asks how much did the man keep.

ANDREW MURRAY

THE MAN GOD CALLED A "FOOL"

ė XTRA One day Jesus told a parable about a rich man who kept getting richer, until he hardly knew what to do with all his riches. But that was just the beginning of his problems. His story begins:

The ground of a certain rich man yielded plentifully. And he thought within himself, saying, "What shall I do, since I have no room to store my crops?" So he said, "I will do this: I will pull down my barns and build greater, and there I will store all my crops and my goods. And I will say to my soul, 'Soul, you have many goods laid up for many years; take your ease; eat, drink, and be merry.'" (Luke 12:16–19)

His solution seemed sensible—build more storage, take more time off, and pursue more pleasure.

Do you recognize this scenario? The man in Jesus' story was both successful and wise by Wall Street standards. But Jesus ended His story with a shocking pronouncement:

But God said to him, "Fool! This night your soul will be required of you; then whose will those things be which you have provided?" So is he who lays up treasure for himself, and is not rich toward God. (vv. 20–21)

Jesus isn't teaching here against personal ownership or the wisdom of growing one's personal assets. Instead He's saying, "No matter how much you store up on earth, you're a fool if you don't store up in eternity!" And the only way to do that is to be "rich toward God" while you're living on earth.

SAFE DEPOSIT

Where your treasure is, there your heart will be also.
MATTHEW 6:21

6. HOW IS FAITHFUL STEWARDSHIP REWARDED IN ETERNITY?

Jesus reveals that faithful stewardship of our time, talent, and treasure will directly affect our experience of heaven.

1. Read 1 Corinthians 4:2. How does Paul describe a steward's main responsibility?

2. Read Luke 16:11–13. Jesus contrasts _____ of earth with _____ riches of heaven. What does this say to you about the nature of treasure in heaven?

3. Jesus teaches that if we are _____ on earth with the treasure that belongs to Him, we will be _____ treasure in heaven that is our own.

4. Rate your beliefs about your money and possessions:

❑ All of it is mine.	❑ Most of it is mine, except the part I give or tithe to God.	❑ Most of it is God's, except what I keep for myself.	❑ All of it is on loan from God.

5. In the Parable of the Minas and Parable of the Talents (Luke 19:17 and Matthew 25:21, 23), what is the reward for faithful service?

6. The reward for faithful service on earth is more responsibility in heaven. But ruling in heaven will have nothing in common with the corruption and manipulation we associate with the use of power on earth. Read Matthew 20:25–28. How does Jesus define greatness in God's kingdom?

"" TALK POINT ""

Why is it so hard to imagine that in heaven you will not just exist, but live a full, exciting, productive life?

Based on how you are stewarding your time, talents, and treasure here, how is your life in eternity shaping up?

7. WHAT'S KEEPING ME FROM A LIFE GOD REWARDS?

Many admit they aren't doing much with the opportunities God has given them. What's keeping them from getting ten-mina results for Him? Often just a small but powerful word: *too.* Check any of the following reasons that apply to you and let God's Word show you the truth. Then write a new breakthrough belief below.

❑ I'M TOO BUSY. *"I'm so busy, I don't know how I could possibly do more for God than I am right now."* Luke 10:38–42; Romans 12:1–2; 1 Corinthians 9:24–27; Colossians 3:17, 23.

❑ I'M TOO LATE. *"It's too late for me to try to become a ten-mina servant for God. I've wasted all my best opportunities."* Galatians 6:9–10; Ephesians 5:15–17; Philippians 1:6; Hebrews 3:12–15.

❑ I'M TOO AFRAID. *"I've had my minas tucked safely away for so many years, I'm terrified to take them out and use them."* Acts 4:13; Romans 8:29, 31, 35–39; Philippians 4:12–13; 2 Timothy 1:7.

❑ I'M TOO DOUBTFUL. *"I have a hard time believing that God will really ever return. The day of accountability seems so far away."* Matthew 24:36–44; Luke 12:35–48; 1 Thessalonians 4:16–18; 2 Peter 3:3–4, 8–14.

❑ I'M TOO ORDINARY. *"I just don't see myself ever accomplishing great things for God. If only He'd given me more to work with."* Romans 12:4–8; 1 Corinthians 1:27–30; 2 Corinthians 12:8–10; 13:4.

MY NEW BREAKTHROUGH BELIEF:
I can start living today for God's wonderful reward in heaven because...

_____

_____

_____

_____

LIVING FOR WHAT LASTS
A Change of Citizenship

"We do not look at the things which are seen, but at the things which are not seen," wrote Paul. "For the things which are seen are temporary, but the things which are not seen are eternal" (2 Corinthians 4:18). Friend, I believe that God is asking you to make a life-changing decision before you leave this study. Think of it as a change of citizenship—from temporary to eternal, from earth to heaven. The apostle Paul, though he was proud to be both a Jew and a Roman citizen, purposefully chose to think of himself as a citizen of heaven (Philippians 3:20). That belief occupied his thoughts, shaped his values, and ordered the use of his time.

Think back over the four weeks of our study. In your own words, write down some of your key new beliefs and motivations. Then sign your name to your new citizenship.

1. *My future life in heaven:*

   _____

   _____

2. *My reward from God in heaven:*

   _____

   _____

3. *My day of accountability before the judgment seat of Christ:*

   _____

   _____

4. *My investment of my time, talent, and treasure for God on earth:*

   _____

   _____

My citizenship is in heaven. I will live from today forward for God's "Well done, good and faithful servant!" I will serve Him with energy, passion, and hope. And I will eagerly await the day when I see Jesus in eternity, my true home.

Signature _____

Date

My Prayer to Live
a Life God Rewards

❦

Dear Lord,
Thank You for showing me the deeper purpose
of my life and how it can affect my future for good.
Thank You for changing me with the truth.
Forgive me that I have wasted so much of my life doing what
will fade and crumble and burn in eternity.
Accept my new commitment to live for what lasts.
Bless each day ahead and each work for
You with Your presence and power.
Please anoint me, Lord, to do mighty things
for You in the time I have left!
I want to greatly multiply Your gifts to me.
I worship and praise You now, and I look forward to that
day when I will enter into Your joy and finally be home.
In Jesus' name, amen.

Those who are wise will shine like the brightness of the heavens,
and those who lead many to righteousness,
like the stars for ever and ever.

DANIEL 12:3, NIV

New companion products for
A Life God Rewards™

ISBN 1-57673-976-7

- A Life God Rewards Audiocassette   ISBN 1-57673-978-3
- A Life God Rewards Audio CD   ISBN 1-59052-007-6
- A Life God Rewards Leather Edition   ISBN 1-59052-008-4
- A Life God Rewards Journal   ISBN 1-59052-010-6
- A Life God Rewards Devotional   ISBN 1-59052-009-2
- A Life God Rewards Bible Study   ISBN 1-59052-011-4
- A Life God Rewards Bible Study:
  Leader's Edition   ISBN 1-59052-012-2
- A Life God Rewards Gift Edition   ISBN 1-59052-949-X

The BreakThrough Series, Book One
The Prayer of Jabez™

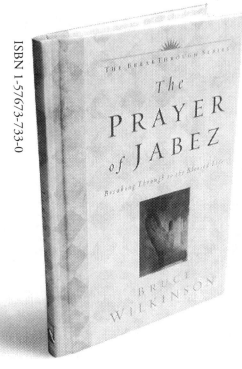

- #1 *New York Times* Bestseller
- 11 Million Copies in Print!
- www.prayerofjabez.com
- Book of the Year 2001 & 2002!

"…fastest selling book of all time."
—*Publishers Weekly*

Printed in the United States
by Baker & Taylor Publisher Services